THE GOLDEN RULES OF BUDDHISM

Owing to the antiquity and rarity of this book, certain pages are regrettably absent, and readability is compromised due to the blurring of the original text. If you possess any insights regarding the availability of these missing sections, kindly inform us. Your assistance is crucial in ensuring the completion of this significant work for the benefit of future generations.

THE GOLDEN RULES OF BUDDHISM

COMPILER-H.S.OLCOTT

GYAN

Published by

GYAN

Gyan Publishing House
5, Ansari Road
Daryaganj, New Delhi-110002
Phone: 011-47034999, 9811692060
E-mail: books@gyanbooks.com

Distribution Network
gyanbooks.com
India, USA, Canada, UK, Australia

ISBN: 978-93-6433-468-6 (HB)

First Published, 1887

2nd Impression 2024

Printed at: Gyan Press, Delhi.

THE GOLDEN RULES OF BUDDHISM
Author: COMPILER-H.S.OLCOTT

ADYAR PAMPHLETS

No. 85

The Golden Rules of Buddhism

COMPILED BY

H. S. OLCOTT

(First printed as a pamphlet in 1887; Second edition, 1891; Third edition, 1902)

January 1918

THEOSOPHICAL PUBLISHING HOUSE

ADYAR, MADRAS, INDIA

CERTIFICATE

MALIGAKANDA,

November 27, 1887

I HAVE read Colonel Olcott's compilation of moral precepts from the Buḍḍhist Scriptures, and recommend the same as a book of instruction for Buḍḍhist youth.

H. SUMANGALA,

High Priest

PREFACE

The too prevalent ignorance among even adult Sinhalese Buḍḍhists of the ethical code of their religion leads me to issue this little compilation. Similar moral precepts exist by hundreds in the Buḍḍhist Scriptures; where, also, all the present quotations will be found in the places indicated. They should be committed to memory and practised by parents and taught to their children, especially when the latter are being educated under anti-Buḍḍhistic influences.

Orientalists and other impartial persons admit that no religion in the world contains a more sublime system of moral rules than Buḍḍhism, but if we wish this to become known to Buḍḍhist children, we adult Buḍḍhists must take the task upon ourselves. Many a Buḍḍhist boy has been "converted" to Christianity, or otherwise brought to despise his ancestral religion, from ignorance of its merits.

Adyar, Madras H. S. O.

17th *November*, 1887.

AUTHORS CONSULTED

VINAYA TEXTS	Davids and Oldenberg.
BUDDHIST LITERATURE IN CHINA.	Beal.
CATENA OF BUDDHIST SCRIPTURES.	Beal.
BUDDHAGHOSHA'S PARABLES. .	Rogers.
BUDDHIST BIRTH STORIES . .	Fausboll and Davids.
LEGEND OF GAUDAMA . .	Bigandet.
CHINESE BUDDHISM . . .	Edkins.
KALPA SŪTRA AND NAVA TATTVA.	Stevenson.
BUDDHA AND EARLY BUDDHISM.	Lillie.
SUTTA NIPĀTA	Sir Coomara Swamy.
NĀGĀNANDA	Boyd.
KUSA JĀTAKA	Steele.
BUDDHISM	Davids.
DHAMMAPADA	Beal.
ROMANTIC HISTORY OF BUDDHA.	Beal.
UDĀNAVARGA	Rockhill.
TWELVE JAPANESE BUDDHIST SECTS.	B. Nanjio.

My BUDDHIST CATECHISM was compiled from the same excellent translations.

The Golden Rules of Buddhism

MERITS AND DEMERITS

LET him [the householder] not destroy, or cause to be destroyed, any life at all, *or sanction the acts of those who do so.*[1] Let him refrain from even hurting any creature,[2] both those that are strong, and those that tremble in the world.

(*Ḍhammika Suṭṭa*, v. 19)

A disciple then knowing [the Law] should refrain from *stealing anything* at any place; should not cause another to steal anything, should not consent to the acts of those who steal anything, should avoid every kind of theft.

(*Dhammika Suṭṭa*, v. 20)

A wise man should avoid unchastity as if it were a burning pit of live coals. One who is not able

[1] One who buys butcher's meat or poultry violates this gāthā. For by paying the butcher for meat he has killed, the buyer shares his sin by "sanctioning" his act.

[2] An inaccurate expression, adopted from Christian writers. A "creature" is something created (by God), but Buddhists regard all living organisms as evolved by due process of natural law.

to live in a state of celibacy should not commit adultery.[1]

(*Ḍhammika Suṭṭa*, *v.* 21)

Four things does a reckless man obtain who covets his neighbour's wife—a bad reputation; an uncomfortable bed; thirdly, punishment; lastly, future torment.

(*Ḍhammapaḍa*, *v.* 309)

Of all the lusts and desires, there is none so powerful as sexual inclination. This is so strong that there is no other worth speaking of beyond it. . . . Lust and desire, in respect of a man, are like a person who takes a lighted torch and runs with it against the wind.

(*Sūṭra of the 42 Sections*, Beal's *Catena*, p. 198)

When one is come to a royal assembly [*i.e.*, any official inquiry], he should not tell lies to anyone, or cause any to tell lies, or consent to the acts of those who tell lies; he should avoid every kind of untruth.

(*Ḍhammika Suṭṭa*, *v.* 22)

The householder who delights in the Law should not indulge in intoxicating drinks [or stupefying drugs], should not cause others to drink, should not

[1] The history of all monastic establishments shows that there are persons temperamentally unfit for celibate life, and whose lapses bring great scandal upon their orders. The Saṅgha has not escaped this misery, offenders having been noted even in our Lord's own time. Yet the general blamelessness of Buddhist monks has been acknowledged even by clerical opponents. A true regard to the honour of the Saṅgha should prompt senior priests to insist upon the relinquishment of the robe by such as are not sexually self-masterful. "It is better to marry than burn," says St. Paul.

sạnction the acts of those who drink,[1] knowing that it results in insanity.

(*Ḍhammika Suṭṭa, v.* 23)

He who destroys life, who speaks untruth, who takes in this world what is not given him, who takes another man's wife, and the man who gives himself up to drinking intoxicating liquors; he, even in this world, digs up his own root.

(*Ḍhammapaḍa, v.* 246, 247)

The ignorant commit sins in consequence of drunkenness, and also make others drink. You should avoid this: it is the cause of demerit, insanity and ignorance—though it be pleasing to the ignorant.

(*Ḍhammika Suṭṭa, v.* 24)

The fields are damaged by weeds, mankind by passion; therefore a gift bestowed on the passionless brings great reward.

(*Ḍhammapaḍa, v.* 356)

The virtuous man is happy in this world, and he is happy in the next; he is happy in both. He is happy when he thinks of the good he has done; he is still more happy when going in the good path.

(*Ḍhammapaḍa, v.* 18)

What ought to be done is neglected, what ought not to be done is done; the sins of unruly, thoughtless people are always increasing.

(*Ḍhammapaḍa, v.* 292)

[1] Then no Buḍḍhist can without grievous sin become an arrack renter, or seller, or drinker.

Let each man make himself as he teaches others to be; he who is well subdued may subdue [others]; one's own self is difficult to subdue.

(*Ḍhammapaḍa*, *v*. 159)

Whoever, being asked for what is good, teaches what is not good, [and] advises [another], concealing something from him, know him to be a Vasala.[1]

(*Vasala Suṭṭa*, *v*. 11)

Passions

Hatred is never quenched by hatred; hatred ceases by [showing] love; this is an old rule.

(*Ḍhammapaḍa*, *v*. 5)

Let a man overcome anger by love, evil by good, the greedy by liberality, the liar by truth.

(*Ḍhammapaḍa*, *v*. 223)

Do not speak harshly to anybody; those who are spoken to will answer thee in the same way.

(*Ḍhammapaḍa*, *v*. 133)

Cut down the whole forest of lust, not the tree. When thou hast cut down every tree and every shrub, then thou wilt be free.

(*Ḍhammapaḍa*, *v*. 283)

Not nakedness, not platted hair, not dirt, not fasting, nor lying on the earth, not rubbing with dust, not sitting motionless, can purify a mortal who has not overcome desires.

(*Ḍhammapaḍa*, *v*. 141)

[1] A slave.

If a man becomes fat and a great eater, if he is sleepy and rolls himself about, that fool, like a hog fed on slops, is born again and again.

(*Ḍhammapaḍa*, *v*. 325)

The avaricious go not to the world of the gods [ḍevas], for the fool commends not charity.

(*Uḍānavarga*, x, *v*. 2)

He who holds back rising anger like a rolling chariot, him I call a real driver; other people are but holders of the reins.

(*Ḍhammapaḍa*, *v*. 222)

A wicked man who reproaches a virtuous one, is like one who looks up and spits at the sky; the spittle soils not the sky, but comes back and defiles his own person. So again, he is like one who flings dirt at another when wind is contrary; the dirt does but return on him who threw it. The virtuous man cannot be hurt, the misery that the other would inflict comes back on himself.

(*Sūṭra of the 42 Sections*, Beal's *Catena*, p. 193)

The fool who is angered and who thinks to triumph by using abusive language, is always vanquished by him whose words are patient.

(*Uḍānavarga*, xx, *v*. 14)

The fault of others is easily perceived, but that of oneself is difficult to perceive; the faults of others one lays open as much as possible, but one's own fault one hides, as a cheat hides the bad die from the gambler.

If a man looks after the faults of others, and is always inclined to detract, his own weakness will grow.

(*Dhammapada*, v. 252; 253)

What is called "Name" or "Tribe," in the world, arises from usage only. It is adopted here and there by common consent.

It comes from long and uninterrupted usage, and from the false belief of the ignorant.

(*Vāsettha Sutta*, v. 55, 56)

Whatever man is proud of his caste, is proud of his wealth, is proud of his family [and] despises his relations, that [man] is a cause of suffering loss.

(*Parābhava Sutta*, v. 14)

Anger, drunkenness, obstinacy, bigotry, deception, envy, self-praise, disparaging others, high-mindedness [conceit?], evil communications, these constitute uncleanness; not verily the eating of flesh.

Neither abstinence from fish or flesh, nor going naked, nor the shaving of the head, nor matted hair, nor dirt, etc., etc., etc., will cleanse a man not free from delusions.[1]

(*Āmagandha Sutta*, v. 7, 11)

[1] The meaning of the Teacher is here so obvious that I cannot understand how this Sutta could have ever been cited as authority for buying and eating butcher's meat. Nothing herein lessens the force of the positive instruction in the *Dhammika Sutta* (*v. ante*) to abstain both from destroying, causing to be destroyed, or *sanctioning the acts of those who destroy the life of any being*. I know a large and increasing number of Sinhalese indulge in meat-eating, and quiet their consciences by quoting the above gāthās; and I have listened with amusement to the sophistical argument that the sin of the killing is with the butcher and not with his sanctioning and abetting customer. Still, I must hold to my opinion until the problematical future time when black shall be proved white.

Associates and Friends

He, who walks in the company of fools, suffers a long way; company with fools, as with an enemy, is always painful; company with the wise is pleasure like meeting with kinsfolk.

(*Ḍhammapaḍa*, *v*. 207)

Therefore one ought to follow the wise, the intelligent, the learned, the much-enduring, the dutiful, one ought to follow a good and wise man as the moon follows the path of the stars.

(*Ḍhammapaḍa*, *v*. 208)

Good people shine from afar like the snowy mountains [the Himālayās]; bad people are not seen, like arrows shot at night.

(*Ḍhammapaḍa*, *v*. 304)

If a traveller does not meet with one who is his better, or equal, let him firmly keep his solitary journey; there is no companionship with a fool.

(*Ḍhammapaḍa*, *v*. 61)

If any intelligent person be associated for even one moment with a wise man, he will soon perceive the fact.

(*Ḍhammapaḍa*, *v*. 65)

Parents, Teachers and Children

Parents should:

1. Restrain their children from vice.
2. Train them in virtue.
3. Have them taught arts and sciences.

4. Provide them with suitable wives or husbands.
5. Give them an inheritance.

The child should say:

1. I will support them who supported me.
2. I will perform family duties incumbent upon them.
3. I will guard their property.
4. I will make myself worthy to be their heir.
5. When they are gone I will honour their memory.

(*Sīgālovāḍa Suṭṭa*)

Happy in this world is he who honours his father, so likewise he who honours his mother is happy.

(*Uḍānavarga*, xxx, *v*. 23)

The succouring of mother and father, the cherishing of child and wife, and the following of a lawful calling, this is the greatest blessing.

(*Mahāmangala Suṭṭa*, *v*. 5)

Whoever, being able [to do so], does not support his feeble and aged mother or father, know him as a Vasala.[1]

Whoever strikes, or abuses by words, his mother, father, brother, sister, or mother-in-law, know him as a Vasala.

(*Vasala Suṭṭa*, *v*. 9, 10)

Research Recommended.

Extensive knowledge and science, well regulated discipline and well spoken speech, this is the greatest blessing.

(*Mahāmangala Suṭṭa*, *v*. 4)

[1] A slave.

The world exists by cause; all things exist by cause; all beings are bound by cause, [even] as the rolling cart-wheel by the pin of an axle-tree.

(*Vāsettha Suṭṭa*, *v*. 61)

From whomsoever a man learns the Law, he should worship him, even as the gods worship Inḍra. The learned man, being thus honoured, his mind pleased with [his disciple], makes the Law more manifest.

(*Nāvā Suṭṭa*, *v*. 1)

The Moral Law Inexorable

There exists no spot on the earth, or in the sky, or in the sea, neither is there any in the mountain-clefts, where an [evil] deed does not bring trouble [to the doer].[1]

(*Uḍānavarga*, ix, *v*. 5)

The evil-doer suffers in this world, and he suffers in the next; he suffers in both. He suffers when he thinks of the evil he has done; he suffers more when going on the evil path.

(*Ḍhammapaḍa*, *v*. *17*)

Surely an evil deed does not turn on a sudden like milk [curdling]; it is like fire smouldering in the ashes, which burns the fool. . . . An evil deed

[1] A man can never escape punishment for evil Karma, nor can any one deprive him of the reward of his good Karma. A Buḍḍhist friend asks me to here recall the case of the robber Aṅgulimāla, who, becoming converted by Lord Buḍḍha, attained the state of Arhat. But this does not alter the principle here stated. Aṅgulimāla's Karma was to be, first a robber, and then a saint.

kills not instantly, as does a sword, but it follows the evil doer [even] into the next world.

(*Uḍānavarga*, ix, *v.* 16, 17)

All that we are is the result of what we have thought: it is founded on our thoughts, it is made up of our thoughts. If a man speaks or acts with a pure thought, happiness follows him, like a shadow that never leaves him.

(*Ḍhammapaḍa*, *v.* 2)

Adeptship a Fact

The Rahat [1] is able to fly through the air, change his appearance, fix the years of his life, shake heaven and earth.

(*Sūṭra of the 42 Sections*, Beal's *Catena*, p. 191)

Matanga, the Doctor of the Law, having before this arrived at the condition of a Rahat, forthwith, by his miraculous power, ascended up into space and there exhibited himself, undergoing various spiritual changes, *e.g.*, flying, walking, sitting, sleeping and so on.

Hereupon was a rain of precious flowers, so that the feelings of the beholders were deeply moved, etc.

(*Ming Ti pen niu chouen.* Beal's trans.)

Lord Buḍḍha's aunt, Mahāprajāpaṭi, and five other holy women, who lived according to the rules, "walked on the water as on dry land; others, leaving the ground, walked in the air, or sat, or lay down, or

[1] Adept, or Mahāṭmā.

stood still all in the same element. Fire and water were seen flowing from the right side of some, and from the left side of others. In others it was seen issuing from their mouths." [1]

(Edkins' *Chinese Buddhism*, p. 49)

At a great assembly of the gods, Buḍḍha, thinking that it would be better if his discourse was delivered to them in the form of a dialogue, and finding that the gods were backward to join in the dialogue, created a duplicate of himself,[2] who, standing before him, put the questions which Goṭama has answered in the *Sammāparibbājanīya Suṭṭa*. (See translation by Sir Coomara Swamy.

The True Buḍḍhist Priest

There are four kinds of priests; not a fifth, O Chunda! Whoever has crossed all his doubts, is freed from the dart (of sorrow), atṭached to Nibbāna, divested of greediness, the guide of all the world and the gods, such an one the Buḍḍhas call Maggajina [the victorious wayfarer].

Whoever, knowing here the best as the best, preaches and discourses extensively on it; him [the

[1] Bishop Bigandet, in his *Legend of Gaudama*, and Rev. S. Beal, in his *Catena of Buddhist Scriptures*, give many data with respect to the powers (*iḍḍhi*) attained by Rahaṭs (adepts, or "Mahātmās").

[2] Or, as expressed in modern scientific language, "projected his own double, or astral body". An aged priest in the Southern Province of Ceylon kindly gave me a small silver toy representing this phenomenon. It is called Samparana. (For an account of the wonders, see Bigandet's *Legend of Gaudama*, Vol. I.)

Buḍḍhas] declare to be the doubt-cutting sage, who is freed from desire, the second of priests, Maggadesī [who teaches the way].

Whoever lives in the paths which are taught [as] the Paths of the Law, well trained, possessed of a good memory, him they call the third priest, Maggajīvī [who follows the blameless paths].

He who, putting on the garb of well conducted men,[1] [yet rushes] forward [to acquire different objects], and brings disgrace on families, [and being] forward, hypocritical, ill-trained, babbling, walks in the garden of good men, is a Maggadūsī [who defiles the way].

(*Chunḍa Suṭṭa*)

Whoever, not being a sanctified person, pretends to be a saint, he indeed is the lowest Vasala,[2] the thief in all worlds, including that of Brahmā.

(*Vasala Suṭṭa, v.* 20)

A priest fond of quarrelling—hemmed in by the attributes of ignorance, understands not the advice [given by others], nor the Law preached by Buḍḍha;

Led away by ignorance, he knows not that quarrelling is injurious to those whose hearts are practised in religion, and that it is sinful, [and] a road to hell.

Such a priest, going to hell, flits [thence] from womb to womb,[3] from darkess to darkness, [and] certainly meets with affliction.

(*Ḍhammachariya Suṭṭa, v.* 3, 4, 5)

[1] The robes of the Buḍḍhist monk.

[2] A slave.

[3] In constant rebirths.

Of old there were only three diseases [*viz.*], desire, want of food, decay. Owing to the killing of cattle there sprang ninety-eight diseases.

This old sin of injuring [living beings] has come down [to this day]. Innocent cows are killed. Priests have fallen off from their virtues.

Thus this old [and] mean act is despised by the wise. Men despise a priest in whom such vice is found.

(*Brāhmaṇaḍhammika Suṭṭa*, *v.* 29, 30, 31)

Some fortify themselves for controversy. We praise not those small-minded persons; temptations from here and there are made to cling to them and they certainly send their minds very far away when engaged in it.

(*Ḍhammika Suṭṭa*, *v.* 15)

The priest who, like one who seeks flowers on fig-trees, has not found any more good in repeated births, gives up Orapara,[1] as a snake [casts off its] decayed, old skin.

The priest in whose heart there are no feelings of anger [and] who likewise has gone past merit and demerit, gives up Orapara, etc.

(*Uraga Suṭṭa*, *v.* 5, 6)

Many men whose shoulders are covered with the orange robes are ill-conditioned and unrestrained; such evil-doers by their evil deeds go to hell.

(*Ḍhammapaḍa*, *v.* 307)

He whose head is shaven, and who wears the saffron-coloured robe, but who seeks only for food,

[1] *i.e.*, destroys that yearning for life in the body which results in rebirth.

drink, clothes, and bedding, is his [own] greatest enemy.

(*Udānavarga*, xiii, *v.* 14)

He who smites will be smitten; he who shows rancour will find rancour; so likewise from reviling comes reviling, and to him who is angered comes anger.

(*Udānavarga*, xiv, *v.* 3)

Those foolish priests who know not the holy law, though this life be brief, in the foolishness of their hearts they give themselves to wrangling.

(*Udānavarga*, xiv, *v.* 4)

"He abused me, he reviled me, he beat me, he subdued me"; he who keeps this in his mind, and who feels resentment, will find no peace.

(*Dhammapada*, xiv, *v.* 4)

Like a beautiful flower full of colour but without scent, are the fine but fruitless words of him who does not act accordingly.

(*Dhammapada*, *v.* 51)

One is the road that leads to Wealth, another the road that leads to Nirvāṇa.

(*Dhammapada*, *v.* 75)

If a man consorting with me [Buddha] does not conform his life to my commandments, what benefit will ten thousand precepts be to him?

(*Sūtra of the 42 Sections*, Beal's *Catena*, p. 202)

Better it would be that a man should eat a lump of flaming iron than that one who is unrestrained and who has broken his vows should live on the charity of the land.

(*Uḍānavarga*, ix, *v.* 2)

If thou hast done evil deeds, or if thou wouldst do them, thou mayest arise and run where'er thou wilt, but thou canst not free thyself of thy suffering.

(*Uḍānavarga*, ix, *v.* 4)

The thoughtless man, even if he can recite many gāthās, but is not a doer of the law, has no part in the priesthood, but is like a cowherd counting the cows of others.

(*Ḍhammapaḍa*, *v.* 19)

Who is the good man? The religious man only is good. Who is the great man? He who is strongest in the exercise of patience. He who patiently endures injury, and maintains a blameless life—he is a man indeed!

(*Sūṭra of the 42 Sections*, Beal's *Catena*, p. 196.)

When a fire is placed under a pot, and the water within it made to boil, then whoever looks down upon it will see no shadow of himself. So the three poisons (covetousness, anger, delusion), and the five obscurities (envy, passion, sloth, vacillation, unbelief) which embrace it, effectually prevent one attaining supreme reason.

(*Sūṭra of the 42 Sections*, Beal's *Catena*, p. 196)

A man who is under the influence of religious principle may be compared to a single warrior opposed to ten thousand in a fight.

(*Sūṭra of the 42 Sections*, Beal's *Catena*, p. 200)

If one man conquer in battle a thousand times thousand men, and if another conquer himself, he is the greatest of conquerors.

(*Ḍhammapaḍa*, *v*. 103)

By oneself evil is done, by oneself one suffers; by oneself evil is left undone, by oneself one is purified. Purity and impurity belong to oneself, no one can purify another.

(*Ḍhammapaḍa*, *v*. 165)

Self is the lord of self: who else could be the lord? With self well subdued, a man finds a master such as few can find.

(*Ḍhammapaḍa*, *v*. 160)

That priest whose [ideas of] omens, meteors, dreams and signs are destroyed, and who is released from [a belief in] the evil consequences of omens, conducts himself well in the world. That priest who, not quarrelling in word, thought, or deed, [and] knowing the Law well looks forward to Nirvāṇa, conducts himself well in the world.

(*Sammāparibbājanīya Suṭṭa*, *v*. 2, 7)

Kinsfolk, friends, and lovers salute a man who has been long away, and returns from afar. In like manner his good works receive him who has done good, and has gone from this world to the other; as kinsmen receive a friend on his return.

(*Ḍhammapaḍa*, *v*. 219, 220)

Even a good man sees evil days, as long as his good deed is not ripened; but when his good deed has ripened, then does the good man see happy days.

(*Ḍhammapaḍa*, v. 120)

In fit time, observe kindness, impartiality, mercy, freedom from sin, delight at the prosperity of others; unopposed to the whole world, let one walk alone like the rhinoceros.

(*Khaggavisāṇa Suṭṭa*, v. 39)

If a man's thoughts are not dissipated, if his mind is not perplexed, if he has ceased to think of good and evil, then there is no fear for him while he is watchful.

(*Dhammapaḍa*, v. 39)

Procrastination is [moral] defilement, continued procrastination is defilement. By non-procrastination [punctuality] and knowledge, root out your darts [of sin].

(*Utthāna Suṭṭa*, v. 4)

Printed by Rao Saheb G. Subbayya Chetty, at the Vasanta Press,
Published by Theosophical Publishing House, Adyar, Madras.

ADYAR PAMPHLETS

No. 86

Masters of Wisdom

BY

C. W. LEADBEATER

February 1918

THEOSOPHICAL PUBLISHING HOUSE

ADYAR, MADRAS, INDIA

Masters of Wisdom

THE existence of perfected man is one of the most distinctive, and also one of the most encouraging, teachings in Theosophy. It follows, if one thinks it out, from the doctrines of Evolution and Reincarnation. It is quite clear that if the spirit of man is steadily unfolding itself; if it comes again and again into new bodies, each in some way or other a little better than the last one; if we can see, as we do, men standing at all levels, on all rungs of this evolutionary ladder; then it is surely clear that this process of evolution does not stop with us. There certainly have been men greater in every way than any of us is, those men also were specimens of human evolution, and if they are still continuing in evolution they must assuredly still be greater than we. Where, then, are those men clearly greater than ourselves? This scheme of evolution must have certain definite stages, and it must have a goal. The probability would be, reasoning from analogy, that it has several goals; that is to say, it has an immediate goal and an ultimate goal, the last more difficult to understand, because we can see no particular reason why such a process should ever stop, but at any rate there is probably some immediate goal, the attainment of which would be the high-water mark of humanity as it stands at present. If that is so, then there should be some who have reached it, there should certainly be many who have come nearer to it than at the present time we have come. We have heard of great men of all times, the church, for example, tells us of her great saints in the past. These perfected men are saints, but they are also very much more than saints, for they are men who have achieved all that was set before them. As it is put in *The Light of Asia,* they have worked the purpose through of what did make them Man, and so they are now more than men. They are super-men, and are entering upon a higher stage of evolution than any we know.

Now the system of evolution is that the Monad, which is a spark of the divine fire, descends into matter. No words that we can use are strictly applicable to this Monad; it stands beyond our powers of expression altogether; but we come perhaps nearest to it if we call it simply a fragment of Divinity. There can truly be no fragment in that which is all-pervading, and yet any other term is, I think, somewhat more misleading. The Monad has been spoken of as a reflection of the Deity, but it is very much more than a mere reflection, and to our limited understanding the term fragment conveys more of the reality than the other. But of course one must admit that it is quite a wrong term to use. This fragment then, being a fragment of the Divine, has within itself all goodness, all perfection, in potentiality. What it has to do in the course of such evolution as may come to it is to unfold all this. As it stands, Divine though it be, it appears incapable of acting or working down here upon these lower planes. It needs to descend into matter in order to obtain definiteness, accuracy and a grasp of physical details, as it were. It must already know far more than we down here can know of the infinite, of the higher and altogether the grander side of everything, and yet it does not apparently possess the power of grasping physical details down here, the power of acting in physical matter with definiteness and precision. It can descend only to a certain level. So far as we are concerned, in this solar system it descends to the second of our planes. We speak in Theosophy of certain planes or subdivisions of matter; of these we have seven, and counting from the top downwards this Monad descends to the second only, and would appear to be unable in its totality to penetrate beyond it. It can project a very small part of itself a good deal further down, as far down as the upper part of what we call the mental plane, which is the fifth from the top; it can reach only the higher part apparently of that plane, and there it again comes to the end of its possibilities. That projection we call the ego. It corresponds closely with what some people call the soul. When the ego is still undeveloped he needs powerful and comparatively coarse vibrations to affect him at first, and since these do not exist on his own plane he has to put himself down to lower levels in order to find them. Therefore, he in turn does what the Monad did. He cannot as a whole descend any lower, but he can project a small part of himself down to the physical plane upon which we are now living, and to that small fragment of a fragment we give the name of the personality. Now that personality dips down into matter on behalf of the ego, or soul, of which it is a part, and its object is to return to that ego bearing with it the result of what it has learned to do. It, as a small part of that ego, learns to function down here, to work through a physical brain; learns to act in the astral and mental body, and then presently goes back again to the ego bearing with it the capacities which it has developed. The capacity to respond to one set of vibrations we should call love, to another would be devotion, to another sympathy, and so on. It can all be expressed in terms of vibration, and that is really in many ways the most scientific way to approach the matter. Anyway, this fragment goes back again and again to the ego from which it came, bearing with it each time slightly advanced powers. There comes a time in the process of evolution when the ego has unified the personality with itself. The man then enters upon a special training, and the end of that special training is to carry him as rapidly as may be to the level which is set for humanity in this particular set of worlds through which we are evolving. This particular cycle of evolution in which we are engaged has to take us to a certain definite level. When a man has attained that level he will have reached the stage at which the ego and the Monad are unified, when the Monad can use the ego simply as an instrument, and work through it on all the planes on which it has been developing. That is the end of purely human evolution, and a man is then fit for Adeptship.

All the lower kingdoms, and the evolution which has been going on through them, are preparatory for that of which I am speaking to you, because you will remember the ego descends only when individualisation takes place. That is what is meant by individualisation, the definite separate ego entering into the man. We are all at a definite stage in evolution, some of course in advance of others, but broadly speaking our position is this: Our physical bodies are developed, and they should be perfectly under our control. Of course, we know in many cases they are not, but we all recognise that they should be; that part of our evolution is attained. We have fully developed the next vehicle, the astral body, but that is as yet not completely under control, except in the case of a very few. The astral body is the vehicle of emotion and desire, and the majority of the human race unquestionably lives in its emotions and for its emotions and for its desires. Some few there are who have conquered this lower self and transcended all desires, and live for altogether other and higher purposes; but as yet they are only a few, and the majority of men are still at the stage where they ought to be working to gain control over this body of emotion and desire. The next vehicle, the mental body, is with all of us only in process of development. Intellect certainly has done a vast amount for us, but it is capable of doing very much more, and it will do very much more. Our mental bodies are as yet only very partially developed, except in the case of a very few.

Now when these three vehicles have been subordinated to the ego, the man is ready to enter upon that higher, special form of training, but it does not follow, of course, that the man who has become an Initiate has perfectly developed all these; it is quite certain that he has not, because if he had, he would have then attained Adeptship. But the man who is treading the Path must have single-mindedness, he must have only the one aim—the aim of helping evolution. When the path of descent into humanity has been accomplished, when the man has attained Adeptship, then he proceeds to live his real life, the life of the Monad, to which all that has happened previously is only the introduction. If one can grasp this conception of evolution, one sees at once that our actions and our objects in any one life can be only relative, only of small account, as compared to the whole. When a man thinks he lives only this one life here, of course the aims of this one life are the things of real importance to him, but when he realises that this life is only one day in a larger life, all these things which are for one day only are things of subordinate account. Now such a man, having become an Adept, having attained that goal of human life, usually drops material bodies altogether, but he retains the power to take a body at any level whenever it is needed for his work. I cannot go aside now into the work which he is doing, but we may imagine it to be very much like that which is usually attributed to the angels. The word angel is derived from a Greek word meaning messenger. The angels are the messengers of God, and so these people who are more than human become His messengers also, and humanity is only a stage through which they have passed in order that they might develop the power to be His messengers, the faculties required for such work. Most of them, as I have said, have no physical bodies, and they pass entirely away from our ken, but some of these perfected men remain in touch with the world in order to fill offices which are necessary for the progress of evolution in the world.

Human progress is not left to take care of itself as many have thought; it is being steadily guided, surely, though slowly, on its way; the progress is very slow, this progress of humanity through the centuries, yet it is definite progress, it is after all moving, and as it moves it is definitely guided. I know that the whole of evolution looks a mere chaos when regarded from below, but when looked at from above one sees that, however slow it may seem, the progress is orderly. The attainment of perfection is a possibility which is certainly lying before every man in the course of his evolution, and at any given moment he may turn his attention to that evolution of his and may hasten it very greatly if he will take it intelligently in hand. Very few of these great and perfected men stay behind in order to fill these places in connection with the direction of the different developments of terrestrial evolution. Out of that small body again quite a small number are willing to take apprentices, to take men who are like-minded with themselves, and train them to do the work which they are doing. Those who have already reached that level, so far as this world is concerned, are a small body of men only; you will easily understand that they are men, not of one nation, but of all the developed nations of the world. These are men who, having attained, are free from the usual laws governing humanity—I mean such laws as compel a man to take incarnation in this place or that. They are no longer forced into any incarnation; if they take a body it is for the purpose of helping humanity, and they can take that body where and when they please. It is not of any particular importance in what race they choose to present themselves.

As a matter of fact some sixteen of these Great Ones are individually known to me. I know of many more than that, but these are those with whom I have more or less come into contact, and these I find to belong to most of the leading races. Four of these are at present wearing Indian bodies; two of them are at present in English bodies. One of the very greatest of all is in an Irish body, two are Greek, and three others have bodies in Āryan races, but I do not know what was the place of their birth. There are some others still greater who come from another evolution altogether. So that you see there is no foundation for the common idea that all such teachers belong to the one race, nor do they all live together like monks in a monastery on this plane.

What are the particular characteristics of an Adept? His powers are many and to us most wonderful, because he understands perfectly the working of many laws of Nature which are at present to us a sealed book. But perhaps the characteristic which dominates all others in an Adept is that he looks upon everything from a point of view quite different from ours. He has absolutely no desires or thoughts connected with himself; he is thinking only and absolutely about the work that he has to do; he exists for that, and his work is always in some form or other helping forward this process of evolution; he exists entirely for that, and there is no thought of himself. Now that is so different a point of view from the ordinary one that it is hard for people to understand at all, but there are some enthusiasts, who live only for some great cause with which they have identified themselves, who will be able to grasp the idea, will be able to understand that a man may truly forget himself in this great work. Another very striking characteristic is the all-round development of the Adept. All of us, you must know, I think, are imperfect in our development, that is to say, one side of our character, one set of our qualities, is usually developed much more than the other. The Adept is equally developed along all lines, and because of that he strikes us always as a very wonderful person, because on every point, as it were, he is able to meet you, along every line he is able to understand perfectly. We are often asked, suppose an ordinary man were to meet an Adept, would he know that he was an Adept? I think probably not; he would certainly know that he was in the presence of one who was impressive, noble, dignified, but there would be no definite external peculiarity by which he could divine the fact that the man was an Adept. He would see in him a calmness, a benevolence, a certainty, expressing the peace which passeth all understanding. And yet there would be nothing to mark him out from any other good man, except perhaps the wisdom that he would show. He would be, I think, more silent than most, for an Adept speaks only with a definite purpose, only for the purpose of encouraging or helping on the great work, and he certainly does not waste his forces in idle conversation. He would be always kindly, and yet have a very keen sense of humour, but a humour that would never be exercised in a way that would wound anyone, but only to help a man on his way, or generally to make the man see a thing in the proper light. A man without a sense of humour would certainly not make progress along occult lines; it is a very necessary quality indeed. So, we might say, the ordinary man might meet an Adept and certainly not know him as such; he would hardly fail to be impressed by the man, but he certainly might not recognise his occult power.

Now as to the question of evidence of their existence, I myself needed no evidence of their existence, because I knew at once that if evolution were true, and if reincarnation were a fact, there must be such men somewhere, and it did not seem to me at all unreasonable that one should sometimes be able to come in contact with them. But for you who approach the thing in a somewhat different way, there is plenty of testimony available. We all came into this matter through the teaching of our great founder, Madame Blavatsky; she herself bore witness that she had seen many of these Masters, that she had stayed in the house of one of them, and that she had met many of them over and over again, and was indeed in constant communication with them. Her co-founder, our first President, Colonel Olcott, also bore witness to exactly the same thing; he himself had on many occasions encountered these Masters, and had seen them both astrally and physically. Our present Vice-President, Mr. A. P. Sinnett, gave the same testimony, as also our present President, Mrs. Annie Besant. She knows personally many of these Great Ones, and can tell you that she has seen them over and over again under circumstances which entirely preclude any idea of mistake or error of any sort. I can myself give the same testimony that I have seen a great number of them, and know very closely, and if one may venture to say it, intimately, all those whom I have just mentioned to you. Many of our members have been privileged to see one or two of the Great Masters, many others have recollections of them which are hardly sufficiently defined to be brought forward as testimony to others, although entirely convincing to the man or woman who experiences them. The only objection which is made to such testimony is that we may have dreamt these things, or we may have been deluded, and the reason why it is possible to make such a suggestion as that is that the circumstances of the case preclude us from frequently meeting these Great Ones, when both they and we are wearing our physical bodies.

Of course, there are those who say that the whole Theosophical idea is a sort of fraud, and that we simply pretend to have seen these Great Ones. A great many people are uncertain about the testimony, because they say: "You have seen these people, but you have seen them when you were in your astral body, and you have brought back the memory of that into your physical brain. We do not know anything about astral bodies, we are not even certain that we possess such things, and we cannot be sure that the recollection brought in that way is a true recollection; it seems to us to be very much in the nature of a dream." But since many of us are, and have been for many years, in daily communication with these Great Ones, it would surely need a somewhat phenomenal power of dreaming, if all our experiences of this kind are but vivid dreams. Spiritualistic friends have sometimes asked me: "How do you know these Masters of yours really exist on the physical plane; may they not be, after all, spirits from higher spheres, who have somehow mesmerised you, and are pretending to live on the physical plane?" All I can say is that if there could be so complete a dominion as that sustained over all these years, then I suppose that might be so; I do not know that I am in a position to prove anything to the contrary, because of course on that theory we may be hypnotised to believe anything. If any evidence can be taken, here is the evidence of these people, and many others. These things exist, but there is this objection, that a great number of the interviews which take place happen when we are in our astral bodies, and the Great One in his physical body; sometimes the process is reversed, when we in our physical bodies suddenly find standing beside us one of these Great Ones in a materialised form. You will say that also might be some sort of hallucination. As I have told you, these Great Ones keep themselves to a large extent apart from humanity, simply because they can do very much better and more satisfactory work when they are so apart. You must think of them as great spiritual powers, as working on the souls of men and not on their bodies. You will find that both Madame Blavatsky and Colonel Olcott tell you in their books that they themselves, being in their physical bodies, have met some of these Great Ones, also in their physical bodies. Similar testimony is given by various other writers.

I myself, for example, can bear witness that I have seen two of these Great Ones when both they and I were in our physical bodies. In one case I had the honour of receiving an invitation to dine and spend the night at the house of one of these great men who lived in India, so there at least I had the fullest possible proof of physical existence, and as I had previously seen the same Great One many times in the astral body, to meet him in his physical body was additional proof. In the case of one of the European Adepts, I had the privilege of meeting him in the Corso in Rome. So you see there is evidence for those who desire the evidence, testimony just precisely as you would get with regard to the existence of any other persons whom you had not yourself seen. But I have never needed the testimony for myself, because of the fact that I feel certain that these people must exist, and, therefore, to be told that they do, is only exactly what one would expect.

The interest for me has always centred round how one may learn from them; how one may come closely into touch with them, and be trained to help in this wonderful work they are doing, the forwarding of the evolution of humanity. We were told in the early days of this possibility when we spoke to Madame Blavatsky herself, and asked her: "Is it possible for us in any sort of way to learn more than this, can we in any way get into touch with these Great Ones of whom you tell us, can we work for them?" She said: "Yes, certainly you can, but remember that they have no favourites; they will take a man certainly and make him an apprentice, but they will do so only if he promises to be a useful apprentice, only if he shows by his character now that he will be able to work as they worked when he has been taught; because any man who still has within himself anything of self-seeking, any man who is thinking of his own progress, and not of the work to be done, will certainly not come into touch with them, just because it would waste their time to invest it in training him." For though their powers seem to us like those of a God, they are so far greater in every way than ourselves, and they themselves are so much nobler—yet each Master's power is after all limited. And Madame Blavatsky told us they hold themselves responsible for using that power to the very last ounce of it, for putting it to the very best possible use for the progress of evolution. If by teaching a man they could obtain within reasonable time a good instrument, one who under their guidance would do a vast amount of definite good in the world, definite good for the progress of evolution, then they would consider it worth their while to invest in that man the amount of time necessary for his training; but if they did not think that the man would repay their trouble, then they would consider the time spent in teaching that man would not be spent to the best advantage.

And so absolutely the only way for any person to come to be accepted by them is to go to work and show what he can do without the training, to show himself to be an unselfish and handy workman, to get to work on some altruistic undertaking. So long as he is working absolutely without thought of himself, and only for a cause which is definitely for the good of humanity, then such a man has the possibility of being noted and guided by some of these Great Ones, for they are ever on the watch for those who will take their places in the future. Therefore, anyone may come near to them in that way, but it is not by any sort of favouritism, it is simply by going to work and deserving their notice. The knowledge of the plan of evolution is available to us all as Theosophists; there it is for us to study, and if, having studied it, and having gained some sort of understanding, we wish to draw nearer to them, the path is always open. Be sure that we can reach them only by making ourselves unselfish as they are unselfish, by learning to forget our personal selves and devoting ourselves, as they do, wholly to the service of humanity.

·inted by Rao Saheb G. Subbayya Chetty, a

ADYAR PAMPHLETS

No. 87

The Place of Religion in National Life

BY

ANNIE BESANT

March 1918

THEOSOPHICAL PUBLISHING HOUSE

ADYAR, MADRAS, INDIA

The Place of Religion in National Life[1]

FRIENDS,

If I tried to say what is the place of religion in National life, and if I answered or defined that position, I should certainly say that its place is everywhere. No religion is a true religion unless it permeates the whole life of a man, and a Nation cannot be called religious unless it be inspired in the whole of its activities by religious feeling, religious thought, religious action. But that very general definition would hardly meet the views of those who have come here to listen to something more precise, although really not more accurate. I want, if I can, this evening, to try to show you to some extent not only the necessity of religion in the life of a Nation, but also something of what history has taught us of the effect of religion on National life. Some of you may remember reading, with relation to the want of religion, a rather interesting, because a very significant, sentence of a great writer: "The times of atheism have always been civil times"—times of peace, times

[1] A lecture delivered in Madras, reprinted from *The Adyar Bulletin*, 1917.

with small excitement, times in which the life of a Nation was running smoothly though perhaps somewhat sluggishly; for if we look widely at history, we shall see that, when a Nation has become very wealthy, very prosperous, very luxurious, then the intellectual and the spiritual elements in that Nation tend to become overborne by the physical and the material, and so we notice in history that those "civil times" of which Bacon spoke, and which, he said, were characteristic of atheistic thought, have been times followed very shortly by National decay.

Nations growing over-wealthy and over-luxurious tend to lose acuteness of intellect, and still more to lose the keenness of spiritual insight. It has always been said by the great religious teachers of mankind that it is necessary for spiritual progress that a man should be self-controlled, that he should be abstemious as regards the luxuries of life, that he should be master of his body, and not permit his body to be master of mind and spirit. There is always a danger when things go too easily with a Nation. As a poet once said, "when wealth accumulates, men decay". A certain amount of hardness is wanted in the development of a healthy National life, and one who studied this side of man with some care put a curious proposition, which is by no means without a kernel of truth. Speaking of war, and saying, rather rashly, not being a prophet, that we were not likely to have much war at the stage of civilisation that mankind has reached, James said that Nations would require some substitute for war, that war brought out qualities of courage, of strength, of endurance, of power to resist hardship and to live without the luxuries of life; and what, he asked, in a civilisation which tends to grow soft and enervating, can we have which will take the place of war as a strengthener of man? He went on to point out the possibility that voluntary poverty might take the place of war—not the forced poverty that ruins the body, makes weak the will and breaks the heart, not the miserable poverty that we see around us in every civilised Nation, but a voluntary choice of a simple and non-luxurious life, a poverty embraced, as a great Christian Saint embraced it, voluntarily undergone and not compulsorily endured—James thought that that might take the place perhaps of war, after war had become impossible for civilised people, and that it would supply the mental stimulus which goes with a simple and abstemious life, and prevents the luxuries of life from tending to mental, spiritual, and even physical decay.

Looking then at that historical fact, we have seen that with the decay of thought and the decay of religion, a Nation tends to become over-luxurious and so strikes the knell of its own coming death. We may look around the European civilisation and see that this terrible outbreak of war has perhaps rescued Europe from being over-luxurious on the one side, and oblivious of the terrible and brutalising poverty upon the other. It has made a call to many of the higher qualities of self-denial and self-sacrifice, the giving up of all that people say makes life worth living, and to the great ideal that makes man feel that he has risen above the animal, that there is something greater than physical life, something nobler than physical enjoyment. So we find, looking at religion, that it is essentially an aspiration to the higher Self. The essence of religion, that which is common to all religions, is the aspiration of the heart towards God, the searching for God and God's answer to the searching. Looking at human nature, we find that the thirst for God, as one great Hebrew writer called it, is an integral part of the human constitution.

Many people, mistaking what religion means and seeing the quarrels, the controversies, the hatreds, the strifes that have risen out of it, say that we should be better without religion, and that we should throw religion aside, for it breeds mischief, dissension, quarrel and hatred. But it is useless to say to mankind: "Throw religion aside." Man is so constituted in his inner nature that there is an inextinguishable thirst within him which nothing but the knowledge of God can satisfy. For a time, it may be, especially in youth, he is easily satisfied with the outer things of life, but when the difficulties of life have to be met, when the laws of life are experienced, when sorrow wrings the heart and disappointment breaks the courage, then it is that in man awakens the thirst for God, and it was truly said by S. Augustine that "man can never find rest until he finds rest in Thee". That was once put very beautifully by an English poet, George Herbert, who was mystic in his thought, quaint in his poetry. He put his thought long after S. Augustine, and he threw it into poetical form :

When God at first made Man,
Having a glass of blessings standing by ;
Let us (said He) pour on him all we can—
Let the world's riches, which dispersèd lie,
Contract into a span.

So strength first made away ;
Then beauty flow'd, then wisdom, honour, pleasure.
When almost all was out, God made a stay,
Perceiving that alone, of all His treasure,
Rest in the bottom lay ;

For if I should (said He)
Bestow this jewel also on My creature,
He would adore My gifts instead of Me,
And rest in Nature, not the God of Nature,
So both should losers be.

Yet let him keep the rest,
But keep them with repining restlessness ;
Let him be rich and weary, that at least,
If goodness lead him not, yet weariness
May toss him to My breast.

The thought there is at once beautiful and true. Man's progress is made by disappointments. Just as a mother coaxes a child to walk by holding up some glittering object so that the child strives to crawl and then walk to reach it, so does God play with His children. God dangles in front of them some shining object. "Come," He practically says, "and take this toy," and the child strives after it and exerts its strength in striving: it is wealth, or power, or fame, or pleasure; but whatever it is, the only value of it is in the effort to reach it, and not in the holding after it is won. A man becomes wealthy, but his wealth burdens him; he finds pleasure, but pleasure cloys him; he grasps power, and he finds his pillow full of thorns; he seeks satisfaction in one thing after another, and everything breaks to pieces in his hands, and turns, like the fruit of that fabled tree in Milton's Hell, into ashes in his mouth; and then at last, after many disappointments, having gained value of the striving in the development of his mind and in the power of his emotions, then at last, wearied with all worldly toys, he turns to God alone, and finding in the divinity within him the power of answer to the divinity without, then and then only is his aspiration satisfied, and he finds his rest in Him who is verily himself. And so all the great struggles of man, whatever they may be, are really struggles to find Brahman, who is bliss. He seeks happiness: he does well; it is a true instinct although his methods are mistaken; inasmuch as the very heart of the universe is love and joy, inasmuch as God is love and God is bliss, that yearning after happiness felt by every child of man is really an aspiration after God; that is an impulse to progress, that is a spur to all true endeavour; and so the very essence of religion is the motive power of evolution, and a Nation, as well as an individual, can only progress by the power of the Spirit within. That is true of religion as a whole. Any special religion has its value in its partaking of that aspiration after God. If you take the separate religions, then you will find that in a Nation's life, the religion by which the Nation has been built up stamps its civilisation and guides its polity.

Look over the great religions of the world, as we have known them in the so-called historical times, and you will find that each type of civilisation differs as the religion on which that civilisation is built gradually shapes and moulds it to its own likeness. If you take Hinḍuism, the oldest of the Āryan religions, you find that the whole of the Hinḍū polity is built up on its religion. The whole of the mighty civilisation of the past is the outcome of its religion. You have not only the Veḍas and the Upaniṣhaṭs, showing a mighty intellect and giving you a splendid philosophy, a marvellous spirituality; you have also a set of books that you know as the Ḍharma Shāsṭras, the law which lays down the conduct of the people and gives a definite line of evolution which the people should follow. Similarly, you find that side by side, penetrated with the religion, you have the knowledge, the science of the old Hinḍūs. You find that within the six great Ḍarshanas, and four of them are practically given to science. If you take Sāṅkhya, Paṭañjali, Nyāya, Vyākaraṇa, what have you there but science of the deepest and the most splendid description? Some of you may have seen that remarkable book by Brijendranath Seal on the science of the old Hinḍūs, on which I am writing in *New India*. You find in those conceptions of Sāṅkhya, conceptions of modern science precisely, definitely and accurately voiced, with a depth of understanding, of power, of abstract thought that has never been outdone in the modern world. You find the very foundations of modern science laid down there as part of the philosophy of Hiṇḍū antiquity.

Of all philosophy, the ancient Hiṇḍū told us that all philosophy has for its end to put an end to pain. Ask any of the great philosophies what is its object? "To put an end to pain," is the answer; and then there comes another significant verse, that you might as well try to roll up the ākāsha like leather as to give happiness to man without the knowledge of God. So you find that, whether in philosophy or in science, this mighty Hiṇḍū religion has moulded Indian life, has inspired Indian thought, has stimulated Indian action; for you must not forget that I have not time to dwell upon it in any detail, not only with regard to religion as such, but also the right conduct of man, as politics. Some of the other books dealt with the constitution of States, with the relation of the citizens to the State, and shaped and moulded the lives of the people; and I do not know that anywhere, in the ancient or modern world, you will find a single religion that so touches human life at every point as Hiṇḍuism has done, whether in the conduct of the individual or as shaping the larger life of the Nation. In Hiṇḍuism, as in another Eastern faith familiar to you—the religion of the Hebrews—you will find that all that was wanted to make the life of the people healthy and happy came to them with the authority of religion. You know it so well with regard to your own religion. You know how often the laws of sanitation, of hygiene, of cleanliness, of being scrupulously careful with water, with food, and with drink, and so on, come in as part of the religious duty of man. It was the same with the Hebrews.

I do not suppose that you have studied very much the old laws of Moses, but if you have, you will find that in those laws, meant for the guidance of the Hebrew Nation, are laid down particulars of the daily life of the people that may often remind you of the laws laid down by your own great teachers. To a man of the ancient day, there was no division in life between religion and the whole life of man. If he was healthy, his religion taught him how to become healthy. If his town was sanitary and well looked after, he was obeying the precepts of his religion that came to him with that external authority. The difficulty you will have in reading the Mosaic books, is that they are mixed up with crudities, because the Jewish Nation was not in those early days a highly educated nor an artistic Nation. You will come across phrases so curious, and occasional comments so immoral, that you are apt to overlook the value of the other parts of the Mosaic teachings. There are some absurd statements, some immoral statements as regards women; others made a duty of persecution : if a man did not follow the law of the Hebrew deity, then he was to be slain. Those are blots that belong rather to the nature of the people, I think, than to the teachings of their Prophet, just as you will find occasionally in the laws of Manu phrases which are impossible to accept as coming from the real writer of those valuable laws of a Nation. All ancient books are subject to that difficulty. You must use intelligence in reading them, and you must learn to discriminate between the words of the Sage and that which is very often the gloss of a later commentator who, in order to serve the purpose of the moment, wrote into the original manuscript something which was useful for the time, as he thought, but was utterly out of accord with the ancient teaching that he injured and lowered in the minds of the thoughtful.

You may turn from Hinḍuism and take other religions which, one after another, had a National life based upon them. The second great religion that followed on Hinḍuism, going further west along the border of the Mediterranean, in Egypt, Cyprus, etc., was a religion peculiarly scientific in its nature. The Egyptian religion was based on the knowledge of the physical world and of the physical body of man. Very much of your own Hatha Yoga is closely connected with a similar form of Yoga among the Egyptians. They studied the body of man in relation to the body of the universe, and found out the relations between the parts of the human body and the larger parts of the great organism of the solar system. Those of you who have studied the deeper thoughts of Hatha Yoga will find that the line of thought and practice is familiar in many of the Ṭanṭras. It almost seems as though Hinḍuism were the parent religion of the religions of the West, as the Āryan ethnological stock is the parent of all the emigrations that went out westward. You find in that Mediterranean and Egyptian civilisation one more type of civilisation moulded entirely by the religion of the people. You find the Science that made the precision of Egypt the marvel of the world, and made their priests able to perform so-called miracles, which were simply the utilisation of some of the generally unknown laws of nature to produce results which, as it were, convinced the ignorant, not by appealing to the mind, but by dazzling the senses.

When you turn from that to the better known civilisation of Persia, you find there in the religion of Zoroaster the essential characteristic of purity underlying everything, a civilisation largely based on agriculture, on cultivation of land, and side by side with that, a similar development of astronomy and astrology, so that all agricultural operations, as is also seen in India, were arranged on astrological calculations, and the beginnings of every great season of the year were marked by festivals of the planets, the sun and the moon. Right through that civilisation this idea of purity runs, and of the relation between the planetary bodies and man. You must be pure in thought, in word, in deed. You must be pure as far as your houses are concerned, as far as your towns are concerned, as far as your rivers are concerned. No Zoroastrian would have allowed rivers to be polluted, as they are polluted to-day in England by factories that pour all refuse into them and make them sources of poison instead of sources of health. Everywhere the law of purity ruled in that ancient Persia, with the result of a splendid, healthy, virile people, a long-lived Nation, because they obeyed the religious law which, carried out in life, gives health, strength and vigour.

But when you come to the next great civilisation and its religion, you come into an entirely different atmosphere. It was the religion and civilisation of Greece. There the key-note was Beauty; not spirituality of thought as in Hinduism, not knowledge of science as in Egypt, not purity of life as in Persia, but beauty of life. When you think of Greece you always think of beauty. The most exquisite buildings come from her architecture. The grandest statues are imitations of her sculpture. The whole education of the Greeks was an education in beauty. The results of that on the life of the Nation were striking. The Greeks were surrounded by objects of beauty. Their city was full of architecture, the streets were the decorations of the capital. The Greek was the Nation of the most beautiful forms of humanity, because of the influence of beauty on the mind and the life of the people. Everything that the Greek used was artistic: his domestic vessels, his lamps, the things in which he carried water or cooked food were all beautiful, and the result of that was that the people were beautiful. The mother, surrounded with lovely objects, gave birth to children moulded into harmony and beauty by the beauty that surrounded her. That was the great teaching of Greece—the value of beauty in human life, and not only in outer objects created by the artist but in the beauty of language used by the poet, by the dramatist, by the philosopher. The form side of life had its perfection in Greece, and the whole religion of Greece was a religion of beauty which shaped the type of its civilisation.

That was succeeded in Rome by Christianity: an entirely different civilisation grew up as the life of the Nations of Europe. If you seek what was wanting in the elder days, you will find that what was left out was the sense of the value of the individual. You know how in Hinduism man is not an individual man: he is the man, the wife, and the child; it is the family and not the individual, isolated human being—a far more perfect conception, the conception on which the State hereafter will be modelled. The conception of the family life extended to the life of the Nation, just as you find Manu telling people to look on the poor, the younger and the uneducated as children; to look on all equals as brothers and sisters; to look on all elders as fathers and mothers. That was the idea of ancient India as regards social gradation, and the whole caste system is built up on that idea of elders, equals and youngers. But that omitted a very essential part which was needed for the future evolution of man, and that essential part was given in the religion of Christianity. The doctrines of Christianity, you must have often noticed, have lost very much that belonged to the other religions of the world. The earlier Christianity lost the great doctrine of reincarnation, and so there was a danger of its losing the doctrine of immortality, though men clung to it against all reason and argument by the intuition that saved it. But you find in the history of Christendom that it is man's own soul that is the supreme matter of importance.

There grew up a strong individuality. There is no use in objecting to a fact of that kind which is necessary for human evolution. It was necessary to have a strong individual, and that could only be developed by effort. You have in Christendom a civilisation, not only individualistic but combative, one man striving against another, every man fighting for his own hand. It is not only a question of physical war; but it is a question of social war, it is a question of class war, and you do not find all those wars developed anywhere as you find them developed in Christendom--evil you may be inclined to think, short-sightedly—but it is not. It is working to a greater good. The example of Christ was sure in the long run to correct this necessary fault in the Christian teaching, not found in Himself but found in His Apostles. You must remember that Christianity was made by S. Paul far more than it was made by Christ Himself. It was S. Paul who gave a dogmatic side to Christianity and made religion into a Church—a very, very different thing. Gradually, however, it was inevitable that the example of Christ should correct the faults of the civilisation by the example of true self-sacrifice. You have that corrective in the teaching as well as the example of Christ.

"He that is greatest is he that doth serve." "Behold," He told His Apostles, "I am among you as he that serveth." Out of that came gradually the idea that strength was made for service and not for oppression, and that which you call in Christendom public spirit, patriotism, love of country, altruism —all these were virtues that flowered out of that competitive system which had developed the strength necessary for the next step forward in human life; and strength linked to service is the ultimate lesson of Christianity.

Looking at that long past, then, of these great religions, we see one other had to be added—the religion of the great Prophet of Arabia; and it is there again profoundly interesting to see how that religion corrected some of the faults of the religion of Christianity, and brought to Europe what had been lost by the lack of knowledge in the Churches. Two marked characteristics there are in the religion of the great Prophet of Arabia. You see how it came out in the life of the Prophet Himself, courageous beyond the courage of man, calm and strong in the midst of uttermost peril, able to stand alone, convinced that He was not alone, for God was with Him. That strong Prophet of Arabia moulded a warrior civilisation on the one side, and a conquering civilisation followed in His steps. On the other side, there was knowledge, intellect, and science highly developed. It was the Prophet Himself that said, you may remember: "The pen of the scholar is greater than the blood of the martyr." But for Him so many men had died; for Him so many of His followers had been murdered—He who inspired love so passionate that when one of His followers had been tortured for hours and hours, his eyelids cut off, his whole body made into a mass of gaping wounds, and his torturer turned to him and said: "Do you not wish that your Prophet was in your place?" "No," he said, "by God, I would rather suffer ten times the tortures, than that the Prophet of God should be pierced by a single thorn." Such love was felt by His first disciples to that wonderful Founder of Islām. You find in a religion such as that the dual note of the Prophet—the power of the conqueror, the power of the sword on one side: a military civilisation; the teacher of science on the other. It was Islām that brought back Science to Europe. It was the followers of the Crescent, when they conquered Spain, who brought Science from the Greeks, which they had gathered up in the later days from the neo-Platonic schools; and then under the guidance of the son-in-law of the Prophet Muhammad they founded great schools in Arabia that grew into Universities, and in a hundred years made the followers of the Prophet life-bringers to the western world. There you have the shaping of a Nation's life by religion. Warriors and Scientists—those are the two marks of Muhammadan civilisation.

So looking over all these, we find in these different religions that each moulds the life of its own Nation, and that the spirit of the religion shapes the body of the National life. How does that affect us in India, where all the great religions are now found? Does it not strike you that in the ruling of Ishvara in His world there must be some reason why this Motherland of the Āryan race has living on her soil all the great religions which have been as it were born out of her womb? The Hindu here has his religion as active, as living, as compelling as ever. The Mussalmāns are here the next greatest Indian community. The Pārsīs are here not very numerous, it is true, but are influencing the Indian life by that commercial life which they have developed strongly by their wealth, by their enterprise and by their knowledge. Christians are here, and in western and southern India there are great Christian communities that date back at least to the fifth and sixth centuries of the Christian era, perhaps even to the second century A.D. So that there are hereditary Christians here, as much as most of you are hereditary Hindus. They have a place here, not as aliens but as children of the soil. We see the religion of Buddhism, founded here by Lord Buddha Himself, and spread on to the other adjacent countries. We find all the great religions on this mother soil of India. How will they inevitably affect her National life?

It is clear that as the outer ways are different, the outer customs are different, the outer dogmas are different, we must look to the uniting power of the religions in the spirit of Religion more than in the outer forms. I might show you that, even in the outer forms, they are so closely welded together that anyone who knows them intimately could make parallel lines showing how in ceremonies, rites and customs, they reproduce each other. Let me remind you only of one case. You all know that when your relatives pass away you perform shrāḍḍha. You know the essential objects used in the shrāḍḍha ceremony. You must have a material object, and you have it in a *Piṇda,* and later in water. You must have a word of power—the *Manṭra.* Without the *Manṭra* what shrāḍḍha could be performed? You must have certain gestures—*Muḍrā,* the fingers form a part of the ceremony; the whole of these are more or less familiar. Only some of the younger men, who have not grown wise, think that this is all superstition.

Take for a moment the Roman Catholic ceremony, which is more closely allied to Hinḍuism than is Protestantism. It is no use converting a Hinḍū to Christianity. If you have the whole thing in your religion in a very perfect form, why should you take it in another form from another religion? The Roman Catholic teaches that there is the other side of death, and Roman Catholics perform for those who have passed onwards what you may call the Christian shrāḍḍha—Mass for the dead. The idea is exactly the same as for Hinḍūs. You perform your shrāḍḍha in order to help those who have gone, onwards through the stage of Kāmaloka to Piṭṛloka. The Roman Catholic performs his Mass for the dead in order that his beloved mày pass onwards from Purgatory or Kāmaloka on to a happier life of Paradise—not rice in his case but bread, not water but wine. You notice there that you have two things, solid and liquid, used in two religious ceremonies with the same object.

Then, you find that there are certain words pronounced, and pronounced in the Latin tongue—not in the tongue of the people, but in their sacred tongue. I have often heard young men say: "Why should I use Samskṛṭ words if I do not understand them?" Because words are sounds, and sounds produce vibrations, and if you change the sounds you change the vibrations, and the sounds are meant to produce certain vibrations that will affect the sûkṣhma sharīra of man. A Roman Catholic pronounces his manṭra in Latin, He pronounces the Latin form and produces the necessary vibrations from the sounds of the words He also makes his gesture—the Sign of the Cross—using it over consecrated bread, using it over the cup where the sacred liquid is. You must be very blind if you do not realise that with a little difference of outer sign and not of real essence of meaning, these two ceremonies are exactly the same. They use the same methods and they have the same objects. In the one case they are helped by beings you speak of as Ḍevas, and in the other case as Angels. The meaning of Ḍevas is Shining Ones—you only use the Hinḍū form of description. The Roman Catholic calls them Angels and not Ḍevas, but the meaning is the same.

Supposing you understand that the difference between you and a Musalmān, a Pārsī and a Christian, is not a difference in the God you worship—for there is One only, without a second, is not a difference in your own spirit—for every spirit in a human being is the spirit of God, and there is no other source of life; if you realise that you have the same difficulties, the same troubles, that you are born and die and are followed in your death by similar love and similar effort on the part of your neighbour whose outer name is not the same as yours; you begin to see the essence of religion, you begin to realise that man, in yearning after God and in searching after God, wears different garments, but the emotion and the endeavour are the same, and that Religion should become a binding power and not a separative force.

Then, you may begin to realise that these many religions of the world on Indian soil are meant to bring together into one mighty power all the powers of the world. Hinḍuism brings its jewel, Islām brings its jewel also, and Christianity, Zoroastrianism and Buḍḍhism bring their own jewels, different in colour but alike in their preciousness. You will begin to understand that the Indian Nation of the future is not to be a Nation of one single religion only, but to embody the very essence of all religions; that it will have in it the philosophy of Hinḍūism, the valour and learning of Islām, the purity of Zoroastrianism, the love and tenderness of Buḍḍhism, the self-sacrifice of Christianity. All these exquisite qualities, coming from the one Brotherhood of Teachers, and spreading abroad among this mighty Nation, will bring a completeness of perfection that a single religion, however noble and perfect, could never give, and you will realise how full of insight and truth were the words of the great Swāmī Vivekānanḍa, that a variety of religions was a gain and not a loss. Every view of God is added to the views already held, and so, however infinite the perfection of God Himself, more and more knowledge of that perfect Being will come to India through the many religions born on its soil and nourished by itself.

Rao Saheb G. Subbayya Chetty, Vasanta Press, Adyar.

ADYAR PAMPHLETS

No. 88

Is Theosophy Anti-Christian ?

ANNIE BESANT

April 1918

THEOSOPHICAL PUBLISHING HOUSE

Adyar, Madras, India

Is Theosophy Anti-Christian?[1]

FRIENDS,

You will all know the occasion which has called forth this lecture. Most unfortunately, as some of us think, one of the leaders of the Church has declared that Theosophy is incompatible with Christianity. Now, it is the earnest belief of many of us that that statement is founded on a mistake, and that the mistake grows out of ignorance of the real meaning of Theosophy; for if Theosophy be what its name implies—the Divine Wisdom—it is clear that there can be no opposition between that and any religion which is true, which is founded on a real message to the world. Some of us feel sure that this statement on the Bishop's part is one which is calculated to do much harm—more to those whom he desires to help than those whom he thus assails; and my work here to-night is less to defend Theosophy as a school of thought than to show that there is nothing in it which is anti-Christian, and that for the sake of the ever-increasing number of clergy of the Church of England, as well as of the other Churches of Christendom, and of the ever-increasing

[1] An Explanation addressed to the Bishop of London, delivered on July 1st, 1904.

number of the faithful laity of the Churches who are embracing the Theosophical ideas, and who regard them as helpful and illuminating. For that ever-increasing number it is a painful, almost a terrible, thing that one of their Fathers in Christ should declare this belief, which they treasure, to be of anti-Christ, and it is largely for their sake that I speak here to-night, in order to relieve them, if I may, from a position which they find to be intensely grievous and painful, to justify their position in the Church, to show that it is neither just nor charitable that they should be driven out of the Church because they embrace Theosophy, and so show, if it may be, that in the teaching that is thus named there is everything that will make their Christianity stronger and more spiritual, and nothing that will make them renegades from the Church of their baptism.

Let me say at the very outset, with regard to the message of Theosophy to the Christian Church, that it does not come directly and specially to those large numbers of Christian men and women who find within the doctrines of the Church, as commonly received, everything that their intellect demands, everything after which their souls hunger. Those who are utterly, those who are completely satisfied require no message which brings to them something more than they have, and the direct message of Theosophy is rather to those large numbers of Christian men and women whose hearts are stirred with questionings, whose minds are bewildered with doubts, who desire to cling to their faith, but find their grasp upon it shaken, who seek still to hold to their ancient belief but find it slipping from their fingers, beginning to elude their grasp. And, surely, if there be one class of folk more than another for which a Christian Bishop should feel a passion of sympathy, and a longing to assist, it is those earnest and devout souls whose faith is beginning to be clouded by doubt, and who, while longing to believe, find their intellect is driving them outside the pale of the ordinary, recognised beliefs. And that it is the desire of the Bishop of London to help such struggling souls seems to me to be shown by the preface that he has written to a well known book, entitled *In Relief of Doubt,* by a member of the Scottish Presbyterian Church. For I find here an effort is made to answer questions and to solve doubts, and I find the Bishop of London writing a preface to the book, declaring his intense sympathy with the effort that the book is making, and saying that he has given this book to some who came to him in distress, and rejoiced to find it useful for the solving of their doubts. Now that shows that the Bishop of London is not unsympathetic with those who are in intellectual or moral difficulties as regards their Christian belief, and finding him thus sympathetic, I am encouraged to believe that when he knows the value of Theosophy in solving, in answering questions, he will give it as warm a welcome, will give it as ready a blessing, as he has given to this work of his Presbyterian brother, with some of whose Church views he finds himself unable to coincide.

Now, as a dry matter of fact, Theosophy has brought back into the Church numbers of those who had either left its fold, or were on the point of leaving it. Many, especially of thoughtful and intellectual men, unable to accept some of the doctrines of Christianity in the comparatively crude form in which they are often presented, have found in the more mystical explanations of Theosophy an acceptable presentation of spiritual truth. They have found that some of the teachings now so largely challenged within the Church itself become intelligible and acceptable under the light of the ancient teachings of the Divine Wisdom, and that many doctrines which appeared unacceptable when they had been brought down to the level of the ignorant, to the grasp of the unlearned, become illuminative and inspiring when raised to a more philosophical and scientific level, presented in a new form, it is true, but the old truth within the form. For Theosophy to the Christian world is a representation of fundamental truths clothed in that scientific garment which makes them more acceptable to the mind of the modern man, and is also an explanation of the doctrines drawn from mystic truth too much forgotten in popular presentation, unveiling unknown depths of thought, unveiling unknown heights of mystic interpretation.

I shall try now, passing on into the detail of my subject, to go along the following line of argument: First, as to the essence of Theosophy; what it is fundamentally, essentially. Then I shall put before you briefly, as a lecture like this demands, the fundamental doctrines of religion in which Theosophy and Christianity are at one. Then I shall go on to touch upon certain doctrines where they apparently differ, and try to show you that in that difference there is a difference more of expression than of reality, more in the way in which the truth is presented than in the inner meaning of the truth itself. Following on that exposition of the doctrines that apparently differ, I shall say a few words on a doctrine that is sometimes said to be additional—the doctrine of Re-incarnation, against which the Bishop of London has specially protested. And then, if time permit, closing that subject as outlined by my title, I shall try to say just a few words as to the value of Theosophy to Christianity, as to what it brings as its offering to the Churches, as to the use it is likely to be in the near future of Christianity. Such my outline.

Now, first of all, the essence. The essence of Theosophy is the declaration which is the opposite of, the antithesis to, that favourite declaration of the modern world, the declaration of the agnostic. You remember how when Professor Huxley sought for a word in which to describe his attitude towards religion, he chose the term "agnostic," and he clearly explained his meaning. He declared that while man had senses whereby he could observe, while man had a mind whereby he could reason on the observations made, and deduce logical results, he had no faculties, he had no powers, by which he might transcend the senses and the mind, no powers by which he might know the superphysical and come into direct contact with the spiritual. That was the position defined by this term "agnostic"; for the Gnosis which was therein denied was the ancient Gnosis found in Greece, in Syria, in Palestine, in Egypt, and always known by that name. It was the Gnosis known under other names in other Eastern tongues, in Persia, in India, in China, and further still back in the world's older history, so long as man has striven to understand his relation to God. The Gnosis is the declaration that man *can* know God; that by virtue of identity of nature, by virtue of the Spirit which is the direct offspring of the Eternal Spirit, man can know God—not simply believe in Him, not simply hope for Him, not simply aspire after Him, not simply yearn after Him with that ineradicable yearning whereby the Spirit in man has ever yearned after its Source, but *know* Him with a real knowledge, and in that knowledge find eternal life. Now there I have slipped at once into a Christian text; for when the Christ was speaking of eternal life, He did not put it in belief but in knowledge, and He stamped the seal of His approval on that declaration of the Gnosis that man can know God.

That, then, is the essence of the Theosophical position. Theosophy reappeared in the modern world just at the time when the scientific world was taking up the position of agnosticism. It was because the science of the day and the leading thought of Europe was taking up the position that man could *not* know

God, and was not a spiritual being, that Those who are the Guardians of the spiritual evolution of the race reproclaimed the ancient verity, the old-world Wisdom, that man by virtue of the Eternal Spirit within him was capable of the knowledge of God. That is the essence of Theosophy. All religion rests on that as on a basis that nothing can shake, on the experience of the human Spirit in contact with the Spirit whence it comes—man in the image of God capable of knowing his Father; man, because an eternal Spirit, capable of that knowledge which is eternal life. And notice that the proclamation is that of the possibility of a present knowledge—not a knowledge of the future in some other world than this; not a knowledge to which death holds the key, and which can only be found in the regions on the other side of death; for that knowledge *is* eternal life, and not "shall be" eternal life in the to-morrow after death. It is eternal and not in time, and it rests on the eternity of the Spirit in man which is Divine. Surely, at least, then, in its essence, Theosophy is not anti-Christian; surely in this reproclamation, Theosophy is only bringing to the helping of Christianity an ancient truth which had somewhat slipped out of sight.

Let us turn from that to the doctrines in which Theosophy and Christianity are alike. And here let me say that the claim of Theosophy is this: that it lies at the root of every world-faith, that it sums up those common spiritual verities which are the universal possessions of all the religions that have taught and consoled humanity. You know how, in modern days, Comparative Mythologists have declared that all religions spring from a single fount." They prove it by wide learning, and repeated experiment and investigation. They place side by side the Scriptures of the world; they unbury the remnants of ancient civilisations: they piece together the fragments of the broken tiles of Chaldea; they draw from the mummies of Egyptian tombs the pages of *The Book of the Dead;* they dig up from ancient temples in Mexico bits of the books that were taught when Atlantis flourished, when the world was young; and, placing all these side by side with modern literatures, they point out the identity of teaching, the identity of religious doctrines, the identity of morality, the identity of religious stories and religious ceremonies, and they say: "Lo! all the religions of the world are the same, and they grow from a single trunk." And from that undeniable truth they make the false deduction which is so often mixed up with the truth, and so gains credence, that all religions of of the world being one, and man being an evolving creature, the religions of the world grow out of savage ignorance and are only gradually refined into the loftier faiths of the world—a deduction as false as the foundation of it is true, as utterly unprovable as the facts of the identity are undeniable.

Now, Theosophy declares that all religions most certainly do grow from a single trunk, but that trunk is Divine Wisdom and not human ignorance; that they are in truth identical in their main doctrines, although varying in the form in which those doctrines are presented; that every great religion that has civilised the world and elevated humanity comes forth from the Father of Lights, and is His revelation to man; and that the trunk is the Divine Wisdom of which all the religions of the world are branches, differing sometimes in flower and in the shape of their leaves, but all part of the one tree, the Divine Wisdom.

And now, as I pass on into the doctrines, permit me to say this as a word of warning: that it is the duty of the Theosophist to study these ancient doctrines and translate them as best he may into modern tongue. None has the right to say, "my interpretation only is the true one"; for in this matter every man is a steward of the Divine Mysteries, and must bring out as much of the riches as he can, and present them as part of the Truth to the world. But when we find that in every religion certain truths are found without exception, then I think we have the right to say that that which everywhere, in all times, and among all men has been believed, that is truly part of the Divine Wisdom.

We find, as standing first in the doctrines of all faiths, in the teachings of Theosophy, in the teachings of Christianity, the proclamation of the unity of God. There is one Supreme Life whence all lesser lives are flowing. It is true that in the mystical and philosophical schools of Theosophical thought this is much spoken of, and behind the manifested God of whom religions tell, we dream of a vast, incognisable

Existence, made only possible to our knowledge because He manifests Himself so as to be known to men. But this is found in Christian theology as well as in Theosophy. The unity of God, the One Life, the One Spirit, the One Source and End of all beings, that is the foundation-stone of Christianity, of Theosophy, and of all the great religions of the world. And next in order comes the declaration that this One, this Unique, Supreme Spirit, manifests Himself in triple form, a threefold Unity, a Trinity, as the Christian would say. Now in the Theosophical teaching of the Trinity there is a difference of name, but no difference of fundamental truth. The Theosophist who goes to every religion of the world and expounds the fundamental unity of religious beliefs cannot confine himself in his teaching to the single names belonging to a single faith; for it is his object to show to the men of every faith that they are sharers in the revelation of the Divine Wisdom. Hence, in speaking of the Trinity, we have preferred to use an ancient Greek term—sanctioned, I may remark, by the Fourth Gospel—used in the philosophy of Greece, used in other philosophies as well, as the name which best reveals the nature of the manifested God—the Greek term of the Logos, translated in the Fourth Gospel as the "Word," "and the Word was God". In Theosophy we use that term Logos in preference to the names of the Father and the Son and the Holy Spirit, and we speak of the three Logoi, but describe each in terms which prove the identity of the Theosophical conception with that which is put forth by Christian theologians. The first, who appears as the Will, the root of being; the Second, who manifests as the Divine Wisdom, which is knowledge inspired by love; and the Third, who manifests as the Creative Activity, the Creative Spirit, immanent in all matter, immanent in all forms.

Pass from the doctrine of the Trinity to the next which naturally presents itself: the vast hosts of ministering spirits, the archangels and the angels of the Christian faith. These also are asserted in Theosophy as the vast hierarchies of spiritual intelligences who guide the course of nature, who administer the laws of nature which are the expression of the Divine Will, those elder Sons of God, products of worlds other than our own, guiding our younger world along the lines traced out for it by its Divine Ruler. It is true that with regard to these vast hierarchies of spiritual intelligences Theosophy gives more of detail than you will find in Christianity as now taught; but if we may trust the writings of the Christian Fathers, of the great bishops and doctors of the Church, they knew far more of the details of that angelic ministry than is common now among the beliefs of modern Christians, and in this Theosophy is rather bringing back the older knowledge than really adding anything to the Christian faith.

We regard those mighty archangels and angels as the product of the evolution of older worlds than this, as those who have won beyond the point towards which we now are climbing, truly, as they are called in the Hebrew Scriptures, the Sons of God, who surrounded this world in its earliest beginnings, and who shouted with joy as the splendour of the plan unfolded itself, and bowed in homage before the wonders of the Divine Wisdom. To us, that ministry of angels, far off and near, is a fact of daily life and of reiterated experience, and there, as in many things, the Roman Church has held more closely to the ancient truth than have the Protestant communities, inasmuch as it has ever asserted the keen and living interest of these elder Brothers with Their younger brothers who are treading the Path that They have trod so long ago in the days of their struggle, ere their victory was won.

Pass from that, still identity of doctrine, to the teaching as to the nature of the human Spirit. Now, Theosophy declares that the human Spirit in its innermost nature is one with God. But does that go beyond the magnificent words of the Christ, praying His last prayer before His agony, speaking of His disciples around Him? "That they all may be one: as Thou, Father, art in me, and I in Thee; that they also may be one in Us." The same unity that He asserted as between Himself and the Eternal Father was the unity that He claimed for the disciples of His love, and nothing less than that perfect unity will be the satisfaction of the truly Christian heart who dreams of the day when he shall be perfect as God is perfect—when even the Son shall render all things up to the Father, and God shall be all in all. So that, surely, in that assertion also Theosophy and Christianity are at one in this inner Divinity in man with all the hopes that it gives to humanity, with all the certainty of a final achievement for all.

Pass from these, in which we are truly at one, and let us come to the doctrines which I said apparently differed in Theosophy and Christianity; for here is the crux of our argument. Let us take ifirst a great Christian doctrine, which is one on which the Theosophist is often challenged—the doctrine called that of the Atonement. Now, if the Christian doctrine of the Atonement is to be limited to only one of the various doctrines current in the Christian Church, and made identical with that legal presentation which was crystallised, I think I may say, by Anselm, and was unknown to earlier Christianity; if it is to be made a legal contract; if it is to be made a substitution, in the legal sense, of Christ for the sinner, then I am bound to confess that Theosophy and Christianity on this would differ. But has that legal presentment of the Atonement any right to claim for itself alone the unique title of Christian? Surely, it is not so. For going far back into Christian antiquity, what do I read of as the earliest doctrine of Atonement in the Christian Church? You must remember that in the Scriptures of Christianity the Atonement is put in a somewhat vague and mystical way by suggestions, by hints of a spiritual truth, and not by a legal definition; and that is also largely true of the statements found about it in Christian antiquity. But one statement comes out strongly and clearly in the oldest writings of the Fathers of the Church, and that is the statement, so little thought of as possible to-day, that the Atonement was not a sacrifice offered to God, but the payment of the price of humanity in redeeming man from the bondage of the devil. That was the view taken, that you can read for yourself, if you will study, as you should study, that most valuable library of the Ante-Nicene Fathers, which gives you the early teachings of the great Doctors of the Church in most illuminative fashion. And there you will find this stated over and over again, that the Atonement is the redemption of humanity from the power of darkness, from the bondage of the Evil One. But I do not want to rest the case of differences of exposition on those ancient teachings of the Christian Church.

Come down to our day. Take the wonderfully beautiful and spiritually intuitive book of Dr. Macleod Campbell on the Atonement. His declaration of the meaning of the Atonement, one of the most beautiful I know, is that it was intended to show to man the heart of God, and to show to God the possibilities of man. Now there is a view worked out with much learning, with much intuition, with much beauty of language and clearness of thought, and the whole of the Theory of the Atonement is expressed in that phrase: "The revelation of God to man, and of man to God." Leave Macleod Campbell on one side, though I think his book has not seriously been challenged as unorthodox, and take the exposition of men like Frederick Denison Maurice, such men as Robertson of Brighton, such men as all the "broad church," as they are called, of the Church of England, and you will find that in every case a view is put forward of the Atonement which does not regard it as a mere substitutionary sacrifice, but rather as a means whereby man is drawn near to God, whereby the Christ, in His quality of Divine Man, forms a bridge by which the twain are made one. And among all those varying doctrines of Atonement which now are found in the Christian Church, among those varieties of belief, all of which are Christian, and none of which has been condemned and excluded, among those certainly the exposition from the Theosophical point of view may fairly take its place, and claim to be no more anti-Christian than those generally received doctrines of the most liberal-minded section of the Church of England.

For what is the doctrine of Atonement as seen from the Theosophical standpoint? It is the declaration that the Atonement wrought by Christ lies not in the substitution of one individual for another, but in the identity of nature between the divine man and men who are becoming divine; that just because Christ is divine, therefore by identity of nature can He pour His strength and His helping into His brethren who are also divine, although not yet attaining to His stature; that all that is seen in Christ is verily all that man shall become; that the Atonement of the Christ does not lie in His taking the place of the sinner, but in His being born into the soul of man—as Paul His apostle prayed that He might be born within the souls of his converts—and that when the

Christ is thus born into the human soul and grows and develops and matures until that soul reaches the stature of the fulness of the Christ, that then the Atonement is wrought, and man is made divine, he who was ever divine in essence, and is seen as palpably divine when his union with the Christ is accomplished.

This word "the Christ" means to us more than the name of one, however lofty, or however holy, and to us the Christ is less an external Saviour than a living Presence in the human Spirit, a Presence by which the human Spirit unfolds its innate divinity, so that in time all men become Christs. It is this divine aspect of the human Spirit to which we most readily give the name of Christ; and while we certainly yield it with all reverence and honour to that great and divine Teacher who laid the foundations of the Christian Church, we yet regard Him as His own apostle named Him, as One among many brethren, raising men by the likeness of His death and resurrection into the living and self-conscious sons of God. That is the mystic truth which lies under the doctrine of the historical Christ; that not only in that beloved Son of the Father is the Christ life manifested, but that in all men step by step that life is wrought out, and that likeness appears; that the Christ Spirit in man is that whose growth is typified in the outer life of that great Son of God, and that the story in the Gospels is not only the history of a man—though that in truth it is—but is also the ever-renewing history of every human soul that climbs out of darkness into light, out of death into immortality, out of sin into righteousness, and out of man into God.

Surely such an inspiring enlargement of the doctrine, taught, you must remember, by many a pregnant hint in the epistles of the canonical New Testament, repeated over and over again by mystic writers in the Church, surely that is not to be called anti-Christian. Surely it makes possible belief in the Atonement to many who would be otherwise repelled, and it is the result of the natural growth of human thought and human morality, which does not see the worst of sin in the penalty which is said to follow it, but in the fact of the polluting sinfulness, without saving from which no true Atonement can be wrought.

But pass from that doctrine of Atonement to the doctrine of Prayer. "Do you Theosophists ever pray?" is a very continual question. Now, in this matter of prayer, what I may call the analysing tendency of Theosophy comes out very strongly; and more and more as the Theosophist grows and understands does he shrink from the forms of prayer which are simply supplications for temporal advantages, and more and more does he embrace those loftier types of prayer, which are either ecstatic contemplation of the divine Beauty and Perfection, or meditation, aspiration, the yearning after the knowledge of God, which is the truest and most effective prayer. We do not deny that temporal blessings may be gained by prayer. On the contrary, we affirm it. Only we do say that those prayers for temporal blessings are worked out by inferior agents of the Divine Will rather than come as the direct answer from God to man; that is to say, that they are rather mediate than immediate. And though it be true that every pulse of man's heart finds its answer in the eternal heart of God, yet it is the divine way to work by agents rather than directly, and to make the direct working the communion of Spirit with Spirit rather than the dealing with the lower material and grosser things. So that we should say that the prayer for some material aid or material wealth would be answered rather by an angel than directly by a divine command; and that those countless hosts of beneficent beings who surround us at every moment of our lives are continually the agents whereby the prayer of the sorrowful and distressed is answered; that it is they who are the bringers of the help, they who are the workers, the bestowers of the boon.

But I do not know that that kind of analysis need do anything to make men undervalue prayer, although it is true that we say that it is higher, nobler, more filial in our attitude towards the Supreme to trust to Him who knows all, and without whom not a sparrow falls to the ground, the care of our material wants, to Him who knows so much better than we know what is truly best; to leave that to Him who knows all and who loves all, and to turn our efforts in prayer rather towards raising ourselves to Him in spiritual commun-ion, in spiritual endeavour, than waste those precious moments in the mere cravings after material good.

For the child who trusts the father is not always telling the father what he ought to do for the child, and it is true that He knows better than we do what is good for the growth of the Spirit within. So even though it come by bodily bereavement and by bodily hardship, better is it to accept that which seems evil from the divine hand, than to thrust it back and claim what appears to us to be good; for often that which is sorrowful is but a veiled blessing, and by demanding in our blindness the boon we crave, we may do less of good to the inner life than by living in calm trust in the rule of the Governor of the world. And it seems to me that this is one of the lessons which is taught in that great story, whether you regard it as a myth (that is, as a presentment of a deep spiritual truth) or whether you regard it as a fact in the history of a man, I mean the temptation of the Christ. Although He could have slaked His hunger and thirst by turning stone into bread, and making water stream up in the desert, He thought it more worthy the position of a son to wait until the divine messengers brought Him the food that His body needed, than to turn the stones into bread by the exercise of occult power—and all prayer is truly exercise of occult power and of occult will. That is our position, then, as regards prayer. We know it to be effective; we should not say to anyone: "You should not ask for that"; but where we see the intelligence growing, and the heart taking on a more filial attitude, we do usually say: "Make your prayer an effort towards communion with the Supreme rather than the craving for earthly benefits. And the more you strive to spiritualise your prayer, the more useful will you find it as subserving spiritual growth."

Let me pass from that to a question that I know comes very near to the hearts of all Christians. "Does the Theosophist recognise Christ as the Divine Teacher? Does he yield Him the dignity which the Christian gives to Him? And does the Theosophist regard Christianity as a unique revelation?"

Now, on that point I desire to speak as clearly as I can. In all the religions of the world, we find that the Second Person in the Trinity believed in shows out this peculiar characteristic of becoming incarnate or revealed to men as man. That is not peculiar to Christianity; you find it in every great religion of the world; therefore, from our standpoint, there is indicated therein a profound spiritual truth. As Theosophists, we should not say that Christ is unique, if you apply the name exclusively to one Divine Man; but if you apply the name of Christ to the Second Logos, the Second Person of the Trinity, then no adoration that you pay Him can be too lofty nor too reverent. Only I am bound in honour and in honesty to say to you that I should say exactly the same to the Hindū in his worship of his presentation of that same Second Logos, whom he calls Viṣhṇu; and I should tell him, as I tell you, that in every religion worship is paid to the same Being, though a different name is used. So that, while the Christian does rightly in using his own name for the object of that supreme worship, he ought not to deny the worship offered in other religions to the same great Logos under a name other than the name of Christ

That is the first point; the second point, taking the Christ from the other side, as Man rather than as the Second Person in the Trinity, we reverence Him as a Divine Teacher; we reverence Him as the founder of Christianity, and therefore as the One to whom the Christian soul should turn as Master, as Guide, as Lord. Emphatically we say of Him that He is the Master to whom the Christian soul should turn. But we also say—and here again comes in our addition—that there are other Divine Teachers in otherfaiths, and that They occupy to the millions of souls who worship Them the same position of Divine-human Teachers as the great Master Jesus holds in the Christian Church. So that while a Christian who is a Theosophist would rightly and truly turn to the Christ, or to the great Master Jesus, as he turned before he was a Theosophist, there would be this which would be likely to be in his mind: that others in other religions find the same help and the same guidance in other Divine Teachers, and that he must not outrage their belief by denying their prophets, any more than they should outrage his by denying the Divine Prophet at whose feet he bows.

There is the point where the difference might be most keenly felt; but it need not affect the Christian who does not accept that view that the non-Christian Theosophist would hold; for it is only that he narrows the meaning, and inasmuch as within the limits of the Theosophical Society there is no creed to which assent is demanded, he may, if he will, proclaim the uniqueness of his own Teacher—and truly to every soul of man his own Teacher is unique. None the less do I think the Christian will do well, in view of the hundreds of millions of human souls who are children of God as much as he is, and who crave a Divine Revelation as much as he can do, rather to thank the Supreme Father that He has manifested Himself in many ways and through divers prophets, and not to claim for himself an exclusive privilege, or declare that all should yield reverence to his Teacher. But if you use the word "Christ" as I should use it, as the symbolic name by which all Divine Teachers are to be named when They have reached the unity of the Father and know Themselves as the manifested Sons of God; ah! then you may bow to all those great Beings under the name of Christ, only remembering that in truth They are many, and that God has shown Himself in many ways.

And so with Christianity. We, looking at it among the religions of the world, cannot say that it is a unique revelation and stands alone as a way to God. On the contrary, we affirm that every faith through which a man's heart seeks for God, shall surely lead to the finding of Him; that there is but one God, after whom all hearts are yearning, one spiritual Centre to which turns the heart of every child of man; and no matter where a man is in the circumference of religions, there is but one Centre to which his face is turned, and although the roads be many the Goal is one, and all hearts that love Him shall find their rest in the same God at last.

If that belief, all-inclusive as it is, is to be called anti-Christian, then I suppose that part of Theosophy would on this point be so branded. I think not that it will be so; for I see on every side a widening belief and a larger hope for man; and I remember that the late Archbishop of Canterbury, in speaking at a missionary meeting to those who were going out as missionaries among the different religions of the world, bade those missionaries treat every religion with reverence and respect, for they also were revelations, although he thought them more partial than the Christian revelation. That is right and fair enough from a Christian Archbishop; for to every man should his own religion be the best and the dearest, to every man should his own faith be the most satisfying and the most sublime. All that Theosophy asks is that spirit of reverence for the faiths of others that Christians claim for themselves; so that in this vast Empire of Britain, where there are men of every faith, and more men of other faiths under the Imperial sceptre than the Christians themselves can number, there shall be the recognition of a common unity as well as a common policy, and that human Spirits shall be recognised as one essentially in faith, however much they may differ in the outward garb.

I pass, then, from that point to the one I said I would mention, of the supposed addition that we make in the teaching of reincarnation. Now on that point I only ask you to study to begin with. You will find, as you study the writings of the Jews, that the teaching of reincarnation is common there. You will find it in the Kabalah, and you will see, if you choose to read some of the latest translations of that, that the doctrine of the reincarnation of souls is taught among the Jews; and you cannot ignore the relation between Judaism and Christianity. Nor can you fail to admit the light thrown by Jewish teaching on the early days of Christian belief.

From that, pass to the writings of the early Bishops of the Church, and you will find one after another teaching the pre-existence of the soul. Pass again from that (for it is a question for your study) to the question which is most important to us, and most interesting to me, because of this book which bears the approval of the Bishop of London upon it. In this book the doctrine of evolution for man is taught. You may say: "What of that? every one believes in evolution nowadays." But thirty or forty years ago the doctrine of evolution was anti-Christian, and every Christian pulpit rang with denunciation against Darwin and his followers. But it is not for that that I draw your attention to this point; it is for a far graver question. What do you mean when you say that you believe in evolution? WHAT is it evolves? only the bodies? But that means materialism; because if you are going to accept evolution, and say it is only an evolution of the bodies, then it must be from the greater perfection of those bodies that the greater intelligence of man comes *as a product*; and that is a very awkward position for anyone holding the Christian faith to take up. How are you to deal with it? WHAT evolves? Do you say the fathers hand down better bodies to the children? Well, but even if you say that, and ignore the later scientific teaching that no acquired qualities are transmitted, how shall you deal with this difficulty, which does not seem much to have struck people in discussing evolution by means of form: that for the most part children are born of the younger, not of the older, so that when men have acquired their noblest qualities and are growing old, that is the very time when they cannot transmit those qualities; for the child is born in the youth of the parents rather than in extreme age, so that you would have the undeveloped, inchoate, uncompleted people as the parents for handing on the bodies, while the better evolved, the nobler, the wiser, the more thoroughly developed, having passed beyond parentage, can take no part in evolution—a very awkward difficulty to find yourself in.

But I want to go a step further than that. I ask you again: "WHAT evolves?" Do you really, seriously, think that only the bodies evolve, and that then God creates improved human souls to suit the improved forms? That is a very curious view of the creative power of God. And yet you cannot escape it; for if evolution is to be confined to the evolution of forms, then God must wait upon that evolution to produce ever nobler and ever nobler souls to put into the more highly evolved forms; and you find yourselves in the most difficult of positions, for God is, as it were, improving in His creation of souls in order to match the improved evolution of the forms It is impossible, when once we think of it. The fact is, that the scientific doctrine of the evolution of forms demands for its completion—unless we be materialists—the ancient and universal doctrine of the evolution of a continuing soul side by side with the evolving forms. Then you have a complete whole, then you see the beauty of the Divine plan, which on one side evolves the bodies, and on the other unfolds the Spirits that ensoul the forms; and the double line of evolution, the immortal Spirit unfolding, and the physical form improving, gives you a scientific and complete picture in which your intellect can rest with utmost satisfaction.

But then there is a difficulty raised by the Bishop, and it seems to me a very strange one. Addressing a fairly cultured audience, he spoke against re-incarnation, on the strange ground that, if it were true, those to whom he was speaking, respectable citizens, had ages ago been criminals. True. But why not? Would it not be much more unjust if you, respectable and cultured citizens, came to be what you are without struggle or effort of your own, and that those unfortunate criminals were plunged without any fault of theirs into the mire in which they are wrestling. Surely that would be a terrible injustice. But for some reason I do not understand, I never found a person complaining of divine injustice because he has so much more than he deserves. And yet that seems to me quite as strikingly unjust as anyone having less than he deserved. Because, after all, justice is justice, and what have *you* done, unless you lived in lives before the present one, to earn the position of advantage in which you are placed to-day?

That is the question before which men's hearts and intelligence will shrink, until they accept the great doctrine of reincarnation. For think what it means with regard to those "criminals in the slums of Whitechapel". How could I go to them and say to them: "You are God-created, and I here, far above you, am also God-created?" My lips would falter; my heart would break, at speaking thus to the miserable criminal in the slums. But if I can go to him and say: "My brother, I, whom you look on as cultured and enlightened, was in the past exactly what you are to-day; I, too, was savage and criminal; I, too, was profligate and drunken; but I have climbed from that place where once I was grovelling to the higher plane on which I stand to-day. And you, my brother, will climb as I have climbed; you are no worse than I was; I am no better than you will be. Nay! my brother, there is something greater before us both than we know, heights that I have not climbed, but that we both shall climb hereafter. For you are as divine as I; the Spirit of God is as truly in you as in me; and by the divine law, you shall grow to heights unimaginable now, and you shall become what saints and heroes have been, nay! shall grow to the very perfection of God Himself." Would not that be a more hopeful message for the Prince of the Church to carry into the slums, than to tell the dwellers therein that they are God-created criminals while others, the speakers, are God-created clergy and Bishops of the Church?

Is, then, Theosophy anti-Christian? Or is it not rather a new inspiration, and a new strength for Christianity? I said that if I could I would finish what I had to say, showing it was not anti-Christian, by a word or two on the message it brings to the Churches, and the hope it unfolds to them for the days to come. For there are difficulties and dangers and obstacles in the way of the Churches here, and antiquarian researches undermining them there; the Higher Criticism is digging at their foundations on one side, and men are challenging them from the standpoint of antiquity, and showing the doubtfulness of the uniqueness of their teachings on the other. But you must not build the Church of Christ on antiquarian research, nor on the Higher Criticism, nor on any question of the value of a manuscript; you must build Christ's Church on the living Christ, and not on the dead manuscripts, otherwise your Church will crumble before the assaults of scholars and antiquarians. You should not live in continual fear lest one man should take away from you this doctrine, and another man that, lest this scholar should deprive you of one belief, and another scholar of another. Nay! those things may have their place and use; and the greatest use of criticism seems to me to be not that it establishes the facts of history, because these facts of history are not very important things, but that it drives the devout heart back on its own experience, on the living experience of a living Christ, which is the basis of all true religion. For religion is not based on mouldy manuscripts, nor on worm-eaten books; it does not find its sanction in the authority of Councils, nor in the statements of tradition. It comes from human experience, from the evolving relation of the human soul with God. And Christ is driving His Church back upon that, because it has been built on the shifting sand of history instead of on the rock of human experience. There, it seems to me, is the use that we Theosophists may possibly be to the Church: not to teach you what you have not, but to point out some truths that have been forgotten; not to bring you fresh jewels, for you have them, but perchance to wipe something of the dust of centuries from off them, and show you how brightly and purely they beam. For we have learned from ancient Scripture a fact, which is as much Christian as it is of any other faith, that man, as I said at the beginning, can know God, and that the disciple can know his Master, as surely, as really, as certainly, as they who wandered along the shores of Gallilee knew their Master Christ. God is not partial, and He does not give to one age of the world spiritual opportunities denied to another, and the value of Theosophy to the Churches seems to me to be this: that we declare that the Christ can be known now as much as He could be known in the elder days; that the disciple may find Him, may talk with Him face to face to-day as He was met in Judea in the elder time; that man's Spirit is not weaker now than in the days of the apostles; that man's Spirit is strong, and living, and free, as it was in the days when angels talked with men; and that it is only our want of faith, our want of courage, our clinging to the treasures of the world that perish, it is these things that are obstacles in the Path of Knowledge, and these obstacles it is in our power to remove. Therefore we bring it to you as our testimony, as witness of the reality of the unseen world, that man may know it now as he knew it in the elder days; that we also are children of God and can know God's world, not only the fragment of the physical, but the worlds beyond death, and the heavenly world as well.

That is our message, that our work: to bring back the old methods which taught men to be free of the body; and to re-give to the modern world the science of the soul, which tore away the veil between the disciple and the Master, and made the invisible worlds familiar as the visible is now. We bear witness that man is still a living Spirit, is still an immortal soul; and that man, if he will, may leave the prison of the body, may unlock this prison-house whilst still the flesh is about him, may learn the secrets of the other worlds, may meet the Master and bow at His blessed feet. And if Theosophy can bring that knowledge again back into Christianity, then you will know of a truth that it is not anti-Christian; for it puts religion on the rock of experience, and thus places it beyond the storms which threaten it from research and from scholarship to-day.

ADYAR PAMPHLETS

No. 89

Thy Kingdom Come

W. WYBERGH

May 1918

THEOSOPHICAL PUBLISHING HOUSE

ADYAR, MADRAS, INDIA

Thy Kingdom Come[1]

THERE are, I suppose, at the present time, few Theosophists whose thoughts are not to a large extent permeated and even dominated by the ever-present idea of the Coming of a World-Saviour. Whether we believe in it or not, however closely our attention may have to be concentrated upon this or that pressing need, there in the background is this all-absorbing topic.

It seems almost as though the hopes and interests of some centre round the question of the personality of the expected One, and their own possible relationship to Him, more than upon the character of the work that He is coming to do, and the effect that it is likely to have upon human society in general. No doubt these are they whose temperament leads them to throw themselves into a cause, not because they have made it their own but because some one greatly loved or admired has done so. For such temperaments it is quite natural to be absorbed in speculations as to the date and circumstances of His Coming, and to seize eagerly upon any available information or hints as to the egos that may have been associated with Him in past lives, hoping to find their own among

[1] Reprinted from *The Theosophist*, March, 1918.

the number, and trying to make sure of a continuance of the association in the future. This is a most natural desire for all men, but to people of this temperament it is of vital importance, for, since they judge the cause by the man who espouses it, if they make a mistake about the man they have nothing else to guide them. Apart from this, however, many people have a sound instinct that they themselves can do their best work only when inspired by personal devotion for a leader.

There are others who, while looking for the advent of a World-Teacher, are less concerned with His personality because, owing to temperament or experience, they are more easily inspired by an ideal than by a person. Such people, being themselves often enthusiastic for some particular ideal or cause, be it social or political reform, education, art, or religion, have the natural hope that the Teacher, when He comes, will give support to their own particular ideal, which of course *to them* seems the best possible. They can, in fact, hardly conceive that He would countenance or support the principles to which they are opposed, forgetting that to others these principles may represent all that is most sacred and inspiring.

Now it is by almost all taken for granted that the great Spiritual Being to whose Coming they look forward will embody Himself in one single human personality, one single physical body and no more, and that He will thus lead a life on earth comparable to that of ordinary human beings. The assumption is that this physical presence in one such physical body is the essence of the whole "Coming," and that the test of discipleship and devotion to Him will be recognition of Him in that body, acceptance of what He may teach and obedience to what He may command.

It follows naturally from this idea that the thing which at the moment will appear of paramount importance must be to spread the good news of His Coming, and by propaganda, by organisation, by every possible form of publicity, to create a large body of believers throughout the world. The existence, people think, of such a body of professed believers will ensure Him a good reception and facilitate His work, whatever it may be. Without such an assumption as to the manner of His incarnation the possibility of an effective propaganda among the general public (and most of the Theosophical public as well) would, it must be admitted, be greatly reduced. We may perhaps reasonably maintain that we have got beyond the point of looking for a Teacher or Saviour who shall be political and national and nothing more. We no longer, like the Jews of old, look for a Messiah. Nevertheless to most people a Teacher means a person and nothing else, a visible, tangible, individual human being.

But surely it would be wise to recognise that after all it *is* an assumption that we are making, and only one among many possibilities. Of its obvious attractiveness it is hardly necessary to speak. For my own part I feel intensely the glamour of the idea. After a lifetime of struggling and questioning by the flickering light of one's own dim powers of discrimination and intuition, after so many mistakes and failures and disappointments, what a glorious relief not to have to think for oneself—to find on earth in human form a Leader whom one could follow with unquestioning devotion! And yet, though I look earnestly for the coming of a World-Teacher, I cannot honestly say that I am able to take this general and apparently simple and straightforward idea for granted. Equally unable and unwilling do I feel to dogmatise myself. I have a tense expectation, but I try to keep an open mind.

Of course I know well that pretty definite statements on the subject have been made by Mrs. Besant and others in whom we have the greatest confidence, on the authority of their own inner vision, and there is a certain type of Theosophist who says at once: "That settles the question. Surely you would not back your opinion against hers!" But this, I feel, is a false issue. No one has insisted more strongly than Mrs. Besant herself upon the fact that all such observations are liable to error, and are not to be regarded as authoritative for anyone but the seer. I cannot but believe that in this, as in all her statements, she means exactly what she says, for that absolutely candid and considerate attitude of hers is precisely what gives us such confidence in her. Why do not these good people take her at her word? I regard it as a sacred duty to try and think things out for ourselves, however much one would rather accept the opinion of another. I do not by any means intend to imply that one should use only his concrete, material intellect for this purpose. But I have been taught that by concentration and meditation on a subject one should try to bring his own intuition to bear upon it, and that as good an understanding, or better, may follow as that which can be obtained by the exercise of clairvoyant faculties. To do otherwise, to take another person's vision in place of one's own, is, I believe, deliberately to stifle the growth of intuition and spiritual insight. I would not therefore urge anyone to adopt my ideas in place of Mrs. Besant's, but rather to think the thing out for himself. It is possible that all three may be right —or wrong!

People are apt to think that an event is a simple sort of thing: either it is so or it isn't so, either it takes place or it doesn't. But every event exists on many planes at once. It has its spiritual and its psychic, no less than its physical aspect, though what exactly these are is terribly hard to formulate or to express. The spiritual is the real, the important, the eternally true, the thing about which alone certainty exists or can exist. The physical is uncertain, multiple in its manifestation, subject to all sorts of modification by other physical events and circumstances. The psychic is uncertain and many-sided also, because it is always modified by the faculties and temperament of the seer. But certainty on the spiritual plane does not surely imply any certainty or authority for the mental or physical image in which by necessity the Spiritual is made manifest.

The Second Coming as a spiritual fact of universal significance is something about which, by the exercise of one's own spiritual faculties, it is possible to reach absolute conviction. As a physical fact, taking place this year or next year, in England or India or America, it is a matter to be judged of by the intellect, aided no doubt by whatever "psychic powers" you may happen to possess, that is to say your powers of forming pictures to express on the mental or astral planes your own intuitions of spiritual truth, or of seeing such pictures (thought-forms) fashioned by others for your instruction. You have in fact to formulate and estimate the probabilities from the facts at your disposal. Unless you know *all* the facts—and none but the Divine Consciousness itself can know them—there is no such thing as certainty, and, since the physical fact is, so to speak, but the shadow of the shadow of the Reality, it doesn't really matter so much after all.

The "end of the world" and the Coming of a World-Teacher are coupled together in the imagination of mankind. On the face of it the connection is an arbitrary one; intellectually they may be regarded as two distinct events; yet I believe that spiritually they are inseparable, and perhaps even nothing but two aspects of the same event.

Judging intellectually, as a student of history, politics, economics, and social science might do, I think it is sufficiently apparent that we have indeed reached the "end of the age". For many years Socialists, a real voice crying in the wilderness, have pointed out how inevitably the present social order was ensuring its own destruction. Like everything else based upon the ruthless competition engendered by the sense of separateness, its very essence is disruptive and self-destructive: it is a question, not of "whether" but only of "when," and this independently of any prejudice about what will or ought to take its place. Socialists have given good reasons for thinking that the end was near, but they have gone further than merely to prophecy destruction. With all their incomplete premises, their ignoring of essential facts, their often faulty methods, their reliance upon mechanism and their sectional sympathies, they have, in promulgating the ideal of Universal Brotherhood, pierced right through to an eternal spiritual verity, and struck the key-note of a new age which corresponds in essentials with the Theosophical conceptions of "sixth-race" attributes, and with the Christian ideal of the Kingdom of God upon earth. In so doing they have indeed "made straight the way of the Lord". But besides the Socialists there has also existed for many years past an undefined, uneasy, illogical feeling of expectation among large sections of humanity, from the stupid, well-meaning pacifist to the bloodthirsty follower of the Mahdi, who can give little or no reason for their belief. It may be said that such a feeling proves nothing, and this is quite true, but the point is that the prevalence of such a state of mind makes a change possible and may be even a considerable factor in bringing it about.

Anyone who has passed many years in close contact with all sorts of movements for political, social, or religious reform, and has shared in the enthusiastic hopes and inevitable disillusionment and renewed effort of which they are constituted, will certainly have been brought to realise, first, that no advance can be made so long as people are contented with things as they are, and secondly, that the best constructive efforts will fail unless the ideas formulated by the leaders are such as the public can make their own when put before them. The real advance is only possible when it seems so much a matter of course to the man in the street that he is firmly persuaded that the new idea originated with himself! The keenest intellect and most enlightened patriotism may desire the most beneficent measures, may even get them embodied in legislation, but until the people are ready they will be evaded and remain a dead letter, or else be distorted and misapplied, so as to do more harm than good. It is not the leaders who set the pace, but the stupidest of their followers. So also with religion. We have had the sublime teaching and example of Jesus and of Buḍḍha before us for two thousand years, but in all that time how many Christians and Buḍḍhists have put this teaching into practice? It has been evaded, distorted, and misunderstood almost universally. The vague unrest among the ignorant, and their readiness to absorb new impressions is thus a far more significant thing than the rapidly changing outlook of the leaders of thought which is so apparent to all. There is indeed no lack of evidence, which the student can marshal for himself, and of which a most convincing and attractive presentation has been given us by Mrs. Besant in her book *The Changing World*, that we have reached a great turning-point in the world's history. And now the Great War is bringing the fact home to millions who could not otherwise have realised it.

It may be said, then, without much fear of contradiction, that the "end of the world" *has* come—the world as we have known it, the old social order, the old tacit acceptance of brute force, of competition, of self-interest and materialism as the dominating factors of human life. But from the point of view of the ordinary or even of the Theosophical student, it cannot, as it seems to me, be said that this change is necessarily or inevitably bound up with the advent of a World-Teacher as popularly conceived: there is nothing, certainly, which demands His embodiment in a single personality, except the *a priori* assumption that there are no other possibilities. It may of course very reasonably be said that the signs of the times point to conditions similar to those under which a World-Teacher appeared once before. But this only implies the *possibility* of such an appearance now, not the necessity of it. I would not, myself, for a moment question this possibility, nor am I in a position in any way to criticise the statements that have been made on occult authority regarding His identity or previous appearances. But I do not see that any cogent argument has been brought forward to show that any Teacher is due to appear in this or that particular body, or *any* particular body, at this particular time or *any* particular time.

Indeed, I think there are some things that point to the unlikelihood of such an appearance at present. It seems to me not without significance that whereas the ideals of the old order, as embodied in the German conception of *Welt-macht*, involve a formal and exterior unity, *i.e.*, uniformity and centralisation, the new ideals contemplate a real or interior unity but an external diversity, a decentralisation and a dispersal and universalising of power and authority. It would seem that in the new order there is to be no leader among the nations, but that the least is to be as the greatest. Again in the British family of nations, as General Smuts has recently pointed out, "Imperialism" is dead and has been succeeded by a sort of composite entity. Similarly it is a very striking fact that while the forces of the old order are, as it were, summed up and typified by the *personal* leadership of a Kaiser or a Hindenburg, the new spirit has not hitherto brought to the front any one leader of outstanding merit or authority. The war is, on our side, a "peoples' war," as President Wilson has declared, and the spirit of it is exemplified, not in some phrase like "For King and Country" or "*Deutschland über alles,*" but in the popular idea of "doing one's bit". The inspiration, that is, comes from within, not from without, and not from any leader; and this is not an accident but rather the typical spirit of the new order. Does not this feeling of co-operation, of being "members of one body," sound the note of Buḍḍhi, the central motive of the future sixth race, in contrast with that of personality, Manas, the fifth-race motive of the past? And is it not in harmony with the essence of the Christ-idea? It has been well said that "Heaven cannot fully manifest its will to humanity through the individual, but must utter itself through multitudes".[1] I do not see how the personal leadership of a World-Teacher, as popularly conceived, fits in with this spirit.

Moreover, one may be permitted to say, in all humility, that such a "Coming" does not seem best calculated to help the world as it exists to-day. There is, I hope, no presumption in trying to think out what, under modern conditions, would be the most effective and therefore the most probable way in which an exalted spiritual Being might manifest Himself upon earth. In doing so one must try to visualise the actual details, the everyday aspects, the practical difficulties; one must think in terms of newspapers, and excursion trains, and public lectures and discussions. We are too apt to slur over the details and to visualise a romantic and arresting figure in flowing, oriental robes, giving out wonderful new teachings, vouched for by the leaders of the Theosophical Society, who would probably carry world-wide conviction, but whom *we* at any rate would have no difficulty in recognising, whatever other people might do. Yet the chances are that this is very wide of the mark.

[1] *The National Being*, by AE.

Let us think a moment. If the World-Teacher comes in a single personality, He will have to belong to some nationality. What if he were a German? Or if He were a Negro, or even a Hindū or a Chinaman, what a load of prejudice would have to be encountered and overcome among the nations of the West! If, on the other hand, He were an Englishman, or even if once again He were a Jew, what sort of a reception would He have among the nations of central and eastern Europe? There is no need to elaborate the point. Again He would belong to some one religion or to none (if He belonged to all He would be regarded as belonging to none); yet this would lay Him open to fatal misunderstanding and jealousy. There are some who think that, as a World-Teacher, He would found a new religion. To do so is to incur the hostility of all the old ones. And then think of the burning questions of politics, economics and social reform with which He would have to deal, and the bitter passions that would be aroused by anyone claiming to speak with Divine authority on such subjects. Remember also that His followers would in the nature of the case be compelled by their own theory and belief to accept every utterance of His on every subject as practically infallible and to proclaim it as such before the world. Think again of the newspapers, with their sensationalism, their superficiality, and their conscious or unconscious bias, and remember that they are the only means by which a Teacher in human form can become known to the masses. And this brings me to one of the fundamental difficulties. Assuming, according to this theory, that the World-Teacher comes as a single great personality in physical form, we have to realise that only an infinitesimal part of humanity could ever come into personal relationship with Him. And yet, if the essence of the Coming is a personal Coming, the personal relationship must be all-important. Even in the matter of recognition and acceptance, a real conviction of His transcendent greatness would be almost impossible without personal contact, for hearsay evidence on such a point carries but little weight. And yet all that the rest of us would have to go upon would be: "Mrs. Besant says," or: "According to the London *Times*," or: "My uncle once met a wonderful Teacher in China, and he told me," and so forth.

Does not, in any case, the restriction of this Coming within the bounds of one personality, one human body and brain, place needless limits to the amount of assistance that can be given to the world in this its passage through the Valley of the Shadow? Has it not been tried before, with the tragic results recorded in the Gospel story, and in the history of two thousand years of warring sects? Will that story be repeated? Must not every attempt at the promulgation of an authoritative teaching or the recognition of a supreme earthly leader have, in the nature of things, the same lamentable result?

I confess that to me there seems to be real danger in this widespread pre-occupation with the idea of a single physical Divine Incarnation. The Gospel story is full of lessons and warnings upon the subject which deserve to be taken seriously. It is well to remember, when we are inclined to throw ourselves into the movement for bringing about a general belief among the general public in the Coming of a personal Teacher, that the widespread expectation of a Messiah and the identification of Christ with him, so far from being a help, was actually one of the principal causes of His death and of the rejection of His real message. We are not likely to make the same mistake, but we are exceedingly likely to make a mistake of the same *kind*, and so pave the way for a terrible and most fatal disillusionment. The real "Coming" may be a much greater and subtler thing than any personal Teacher could be, even as Jesus Christ was infinitely greater as a personal Teacher than any national Messiah, and the expectation of a personal Teacher may conceivably hinder the recognition of the Spiritual Coming of the Son of Man. And if we are inclined to look for new and authoritative statements of doctrine, religious or social, let us remember that Jesus Himself obviously had no intention of founding a religion and gave little or none of the doctrinal teaching which was afterwards organised into religion in His name. The Kingdom of Heaven which He preached is an inner psychological or spiritual condition, not a creed or an organisation or even a system of morality. Is it not therefore more probable that the Second Coming will mean rather the deepening of the spiritual life than anything external?

Is there not a danger in leading people to expect *any* specific "teaching," whether religious, scientific or political? What seems to me a thing greatly to be dreaded is the spirit which, in the absence of direct personal knowledge, is all agog with expectation, ready to run here and there crying "Lord! Lord!" and seeking for a sign; and this spirit is only too easily fostered if attention and hope is concentrated upon the advent of a personality in the outer world. Better, surely, would it be to "make straight the way of the Lord" in the heart, by training the intuition, by helping forward the inner change without which no outer Advent can have any meaning. So shall men be able to recognise the Lord when He comes, in the personality of their neighbour, or perchance their enemy or their servant.

And still humanity cries aloud in its agony: "My God, my God, why hast thou forsaken me?" Once more the whole creation groans and travails, waiting for the coming of the Sons of God. Is the waiting vain? Shall the hope of millions be disappointed? If that were so, if the "end of the world" does not imply the Second Coming, I confess, for my own part, that I see little hope for the world. Without some such help from the spiritual world I think there is a very real prospect that civilisation itself will go under, and that a destruction will come upon mankind comparable only with that of Atlantis. The faculties and the methods to which we are accustomed will not suffice to avert the doom. The inadequacy and the fatal corruption of the old is recognised;

mankind is awake to the necessity, not merely of reforms and patches, but of a transvaluation of all values, and real *metanoia,* a change of mind; but we lack the inspiration, the Divine life-giving breath, the creative spirit needed to bring about a new heaven and a new earth. The old forces of desire and self-interest and material intellect grind on—they are grinding themselves to pieces; but of themselves they can never evolve anything new. They work in a closed circle. They can but re-arrange existing material into forms of the same order. A kaleidoscope produces endless patterns, but never a work of art. So it is that the endless efforts of able but uninspired men now concentrated upon post-war problems, devising better machinery, cutting away abuses, excellent and indispensable as they are, can in themselves avail nothing. We are being purged, we are driving out the devils that have possessed us. Soon we shall be empty, swept, and garnished; and then—either the Son of Man, or seven devils worse than the first.

Let us lift up our hearts. Without the Crucifixion there can be no Resurrection, and the depth of the despair is the guarantee of the greatness of the approaching birth. Little warrant though there be for expecting the Advent of a Supreme Teacher as an individual, there is every reason to expect the inflow of the Life-giving Spirit which is Himself. Let us look beyond the individual and visualise humanity as a whole, as the mystical Body of Christ. Let us try to understand its psychology by what we know of the workings of the individual human heart, and perhaps we shall have less difficulty in reading the signs of the times. The ferment which we see and feel around us, realised in a greater or less degree by each individual according to his place in the scale of evolution; the gathering of the hosts of Armageddon; the darkening of the spiritual Sun; the pouring out of the "vials of the wrath of God"—are the symptoms which in the individual man precede and herald "conversion" and similar great transformations of attitude and ruling motive. They are comparable with those strange and terrible torments of the soul undergone at certain stages by all who enter the Path, wherein their souls are crucified, dead, and buried. They are followed in the individual by a New Birth. And Who and What is then born? The mystic calls Him Christ, and with that birth the pre-occupation with the historical and physical birth of Christ ceases. "Hitherto I have known Christ after the flesh," says St. Paul, "henceforth know I Him no more." For the inner birth is felt to be the reality.

And may it not be so with regard to this second World-Coming for which we look? Would not such a Coming, universal, interior, and spiritual, be a far greater and more real and efficacious thing than any conceivable individual physical incarnation?

> Though Christ a thousand times in Bethlehem be
> born,
> If He's not born in thee thy soul is all forlorn.

As I see it, though but "through a glass, darkly," the End of the World and the Coming of the Son of Man are indissolubly connected. For me the tremendous drama of the Last Day has always had a profound significance. Since I was a boy the solemn strains of *Dies Iræ, dies illa,* the thrill of expectation which runs through Handel's *Messiah,* the soul-stirring and overpowering imagery of the *Apocalypse,* have never failed to arouse in me a deep response. I have dreamed of it and brooded over it, not as an intellectual problem but as a vital truth engrained in the fabric of the Universe; not as a distant event but as something which I myself shall surely take part in; not with fear but with the solemn expectation of something too great for expression. And its significance has become not less but greater, because what was once, to my childish imagination, a picture of outer events, has become pregnant with inner meaning.

St. Paul, speaking of these things, significantly says: "Behold, I show you a mystery." The drama of the Last Day and the Second Coming is one that is enacted in the human soul, both individually and collectively. The Second Advent is indeed an incarnation, a descent of the Christ into human form. Yet that which stirs me to the depths is the hope, not of a Leader and Teacher in the outer world, but of the Coming of the Christ into the heart of poor suffering and struggling humanity. Short of that nothing can suffice. We may accept and acknowledge an outer Teacher, but only when the Christ comes to the heart does He bring unquestioning certainty and devotion. Salvation and regeneration can only come from within.

I can well believe that the dawn of the new age may be signalised by the entrance into incarnation of many great souls, but I do not picture them to myself as outwardly united or organised in common acknowledgment of some supreme Head in the physical world. Rather do I think of them as men and women of all nations and kindreds and peoples and tongues, leaders it may be of different schools of thought and teaching, different spheres of action; unknown—perhaps even opposed to one another in the outer world, neither claiming nor being accorded divine authority or obedience: for the function of the Spirit is everywhere and always not to command or to instruct but to inspire, not to redeem mankind but to help mankind to redeem itself.

Therefore, above all and beyond all, the actual and essential Coming of the Son of Man that I look for is the quickening of all from within rather than the advent of specially dowered individuals.

The trumpet shall sound, and the dead shall be raised. And we shall all be changed, and in Christ shall all be made alive. For the drama of the Second Coming is above all the drama of Initiation, that tremendous event which signifies in the individual the breaking up of the separated self and its reconstitution in the Mystical Body of Christ. For humanity as a whole it is the breaking up of the old order, necessary, irresistible, long foreseen; carrying with it torment unspeakable, darkness, confusion and despair, but to be followed by entry into a higher type of consciousness, by the opening up of new possibilities and new points of view, by a greater realisation of our common brotherhood. Far indeed are we from the period when humanity as a whole will be able to take the stage of Initiation which is possible for its most advanced members, yet the time is at hand when a definite step forward can be taken. The coming of the Christ to all, individually, means that each will receive, not in the same measure, but according to his capacity. For the less advanced masses of humanity this may imply a relatively quite small advance in mutual goodwill and the power of response to higher influences. For those who are approaching the threshold of the Kingdom it may mean the power to pass that threshold. The total and cumulative effect of such an universal increase of faculty may well be stupendous, and may make possible changes in the social order which at present appear to be, and actually are, an impracticable dream. Human nature may indeed be changed, for there is a power that worketh in us and maketh all things new.

So may Christ come, collectively, to humanity.

And, behold, I come quickly; and my reward is with me, to give every man according as his work shall be.

Surely I come quickly. Amen.
Even so, come, Lord Jesus.

Printer: G. Subbayya Chetty, Vasanta Press, Adyar.

ADYAR PAMPHLETS

No. 90

The Count de Saint-Germain and H.P.B., Two Messengers of the White Lodge

BY

H. S. OLCOTT

Reprinted from *The Theosophist*, July, 1905

June 1918

THEOSOPHICAL PUBLISHING HOUSE

ADYAR, MADRAS, INDIA

The Count de Saint-Germain and H.P.B., Two Messengers of the White Lodge

To me, one of the most picturesque, impressive and admirable characters in modern history is the wonder-worker whose name heads this article. The world does not see him as a recluse of the desert or the jungle, unwashed, wrinkled, hairy and clothed in rags, living apart from his fellow men and devoid of human sympathies; but as one who amid the splendour of the most brilliant European courts, equalled the greatest of the personages who move across the canvas of history. He towered above them all—kings, nobles, philosophers, stetesmen and men of letters, in the majesty of his personal character, the nobility of his ideals and motives, the consistency of his acts and the profundity of his knowledge, not only of the mysteries of Nature, but also of the literature of all peoples and epochs. By reading all I could find about him, including the instructive articles of Mrs. Cooper-Oakley in *The Theosophical Review* (Vols. 21 and 22) I have come to love as well as to admire him; to love him as did H.P.B.; and for the same reason—that he was a messenger and agent of the White Lodge, accomplishing his mission with unselfish loyalty and doing all that lay within man's power to benefit others.

The recent reading of a biographical memoir under the form of an historical romance, of the famous "Souvenirs" of the Baron De Gleichen; of an interesting article in Vol. 6. of *Le Lotus Bleu*; of the article on the Count in the *Encyclopædia Britannica* and other publications, has freshened up all my memories of what I had heard about him, and, more important still, has persuaded me of his identity with one of the most charming of the Unseen Personages who stood behind the masque of H.P.B. during the writing of *Isis Unveiled.* The more I think of it, the more fully am I persuaded of the truth of this surmise.

Before going into these details, however, it will be well just simply to say that one day, in the eighteenth century, he appeared in France under the name above given. It is said that he had taken it from an estate bought by him in the Tyrol. Mrs. Cooper-Oakley gives, on the authority of Mme. D'Adhémar, a list of the different names under which this maker of epochs had been known, from the year 1710 to 1822. I cite the following: Marquis de Montferrat, Comte Bellamarre, Chevalier Schoening, Chevalier Weldon, Comte Soltikoff, Graf Tzarogy, Prinz Ragoczy, and finally, Saint-Germain. Mrs. Cooper-Oakley, with the help of friends, made an industrious search in the libraries of the British Museum and in those of several European kingdoms. She patiently collated from various sources bits of history which go to identify the great Count with the personages known under these different titles. But it is conceded by all who have written about him that the real secret of his birth and nationality was never discovered; all the labours of all the police authorities of different countries resulted only in failure. Another fact of great interest is that no crime nor criminal intention nor deception was ever proved against him; his character was unblemished, his aims always noble. Though living in luxury and seemingly possessed of boundless wealth, no one could ever learn whence his money came; he kept no bank account, received no cash remittances, enjoyed no pension from any government, refused every offer of presents and benefits made him by King Louis XV, and other sovereigns, and yet his generosity was princely. To the poor and miserable, the sick and the oppressed, he was an incarnate Providence; among other public benefactions, he founded a hospital at Paris, and possibly others elsewhere.

Grim, in his celebrated "*Correspondance Litteraire,*" which is described by the *Encyc. Brit.* as "the most valuable of existing records of any important literary period," affirms that St.-Germain was "the man of the best parts he had ever seen". He knew all languages, all history, all transcendental science; took no present nor patronage, refused all offers of such, gave lavishly, founded hospitals, and worked ever and always unflaggingly for the benefit of the race. One would think that such a man might have been spared by the slanderer and the calumniator, yet he was not; while yet living and since his death (or disappearance, rather) the vilest insults have been showered upon his memory. Says the *Encyc. Brit.* he was "a celebrated adventurer of the eighteenth century who by the assertion of his discovery of some extraordinary secrets of nature exercised considerable influence at several European Courts. . . . It was commonly stated that he obtained his money from discharging the functions of spy to one of the European Courts."

The identical opinion of him is echoed by Bouilferet in his *Dictionnaire d'Histoire et de Geographie*, and by various other writers.

We have various descriptions of the personal appearance of Count St.-Germain, and although they differ somewhat in details, yet all describe him as a man in radiant health, and of unflagging courtesy and good humour. His manners were the perfection of refinement and grace. He seems to have been a remarkable linguist, speaking fluently and usually without foreign accent the current languages of Europe. One writer, signing himself Jean Léclaireur, says in an interesting article on "*Le Secret du Comte de Saint-Germain*," in the *Lotus Bleu*, Vol. VI, 314-319, that he was familiar with French, English, Italian, Spanish, Portuguese, German, Russian, Danish, Swedish and many oriental dialects. His accomplishments in this latter respect supply one of the points of resemblance which are so striking between himself and H.P.B. For His Highness the late Prince Emil de Sayn-Wittgenstein, A. D. C. to the Emperor Nicholas and an early member of our Society, wrote me once that when he knew H.P.B. at Tiflis, she was famed for her ability to speak most of the languages of the Caucasus—Georgian, Mingrelian, Abhasian, etc., while we ourselves have seen her producing literature of a superior class in Russian, French and English. But the more one reads about Saint-Germain and knows about H.P.B., the more numerous and striking are the resemblances between the two great occultists. Mrs. Cooper-Oakley in her careful compilation says (*Theos. Rev.*, Vol. XXI, p. 428): "It was almost universally accorded that he had a charming grace and courtliness of manner. He displayed, moreover, in society a great variety of gifts, played several musical instruments excellently, and sometimes showed faculties and powers which bordered on the mysterious and incomprehensible. For example, one day he had dictated to him the first twenty verses of a poem, and wrote them simultaneously with both hands on two separate sheets of paper—no one present could distinguish one sheet from the other."

Mr. Léclaireur, in the article above noticed, has summarised many points about Count St.-Germain which corroborate the foregoing and seem to be carefully compiled from the literature of the subject. He says that: "His beauty was remarkable and his manners splendid; he had an extraordinary talent for elocution, a marvellous education and erudition. . . . An accomplished musician, he played on all instruments, but was particularly fond of the violin; he made it vibrate so divinely that two persons who heard him and afterwards the famous Italian master, Paganini, placed the two artists on the same level." Here we recall the superb facility of H. P. B. as a pianist, her butterfly-like touch, her improvisatorial faculty and her knowledge of technique. Baron Gleichen quotes him as saying: "You do not know what you are talking about; only I can discuss the matter, which I have exhausted, as I have music, which I abandoned because I was unable to go any farther in it." The Baron was invited to his house with the ostensible object of examining some very valuable paintings, and the Baron says that "he kept his word, for the paintings which he showed me had the character of singularity or of perfection, which made them more interesting than many pictures of the first rank, especially a holy family of Murillo which equalled in beauty that of Raphael at Versailles; but he showed me much more than that, *viz.*, a quantity of gems, especially of diamonds, of surprising colour, size, and perfection. I thought I was looking at the treasures of the Wonderful Lamp. There were among others an opal of monstrous size and a white sapphire as large as an egg, which paled by its brilliancy that of all the stones that I placed beside it for comparison. I dare to profess to be a connoisseur in jewels, and I declare that the eye could not discover the least reason to doubt the fineness of these stones, the more so since they were not mounted."

Many years ago my sister, Mrs. Mitchell, feeling indignant at the base slanders that were being circulated against H.P.B. and myself, and wishing to place on record some of the facts that came under her own notice while occupying, with her husband and children, a flat in the same building as ourselves, published in a London journal an article in which the following incident among others is given: "One day she said she would show me some pretty things; and going to a small chest of drawers that stood beneath one of the windows, she took from them many pieces of superb jewellery; brooches, lockets, bracelets and rings, that were ablaze with all kinds of precious stones, diamonds, rubies, sapphires, etc. I held and examined them, but on asking to see them the next day I found only empty drawers." My sister thought they must have been worth a great many thousands of dollars. Now as I happened to know that H. P. B. had no such collection of precious stones nor even a small portion of them, my only possible inference is that she had played on my sister's sight one of those optical illusions which she described as psychological tricks. I am inclined to believe that St.-Germain did the same to Baron Gleichen. True, these wonder-workers can at their pleasure turn such an illusion into a reality and make the gems solid and permanent. Take, for instance, my "rose-ring" (see *O. D. L.*, I, 96) which she first made to leap out of a rose which I was holding in my hand, and, eighteen months later, while my sister held it, caused three small diamonds to be set in the gold in the form of a triangle. Many persons in different countries have seen this ring, and some have seen me write with it on glass, thus proving the stones to be genuine diamonds. The ring is still in my possession, and during the intervening thirty years has not changed its character at all. Moreover, there are the cases of her duplication of a yellow diamond for Mrs. Sinnett at Simla, of sapphires for Mrs. Carmichael and other friends at different places, her making her mystic seal-ring, now in Mrs. Besant's possession, by rubbing between her hands my own intaglio seal-ring; and the hybrid silver sugar-tongs, and, first and last, many articles of metal and stone which, having been duly described in my *O. D. L.*, need not be here recapitulated. The reader will see that the respective phenomena of St.-Germain and H. P. B. complement and corroborate each other, and that they go to show that among the branches of occult science that are familiar to adepts and their advanced pupils, is to be included an intimate knowledge of and control over the mineral kingdom. St.-Germain told somebody that he had learnt from an old Hinḍū Brahmin how to "revive" pure carbon, that is to say to transmute it into diamond; and Kenneth Mackenzie is quoted as saying (in his *Royal Masonic Cyclopædia*, p. 644): "In 1780, during his visit to the French ambassador to the Hague, he smashed with a hammer a superb diamond which he had produced by alchemical means; the mate to it, also made by him, he had sold to a jeweller, for the price of 5,500 *louis d'or.*"

We have nothing in any of these accounts going to show whether any of the gems made by him remained solid or whether they dissolved back into the astral matter out of which they had been composed, except in the specific cases where a gem had been given to some individual, or in that where one had been sold to a jeweller. To me it is unthinkable that he should have sold the diamond for the sake of raising 5,500 *louis*, for the fact of his having apparently unlimited command of money shows that he could not have needed so small a sum.

We have spoken above of the dissolution of a gem magically created. If the reader will refer to *O.D.L.*, I, 197 and 198, he will see that the first picture of "Chevalier Louis," precipitated by H.P.B. on a certain evening, had faded out by the next morning, but that when she again caused it to appear, at Mr. Judge's request, she had "fixed" it so that it remains unchanged to the present time of writing. My explanation of that is that it depended entirely upon the adept operator whether he should make a fugitive precipitation of the thought-picture, leaving it to be acted upon and dissipated by the attraction of space, or on making the deposit of pigment, cut off the current which connected it with space and so leaving it a permanent pigmentary deposit on the paper or other surface. In fact I strongly advise anyone who wants to get at the mysteries of Count St.-Germain, Cagliostro and other wonder-workers, to read in connection with them the various accounts of H.P.B.'s phenomena which have been published by credible witnesses. Take for example the quotation made by Mrs. Cooper-Oakley from the "*Souvenirs de Marie-Antoinette,*" by the Countess d'Adhémar, who had been an intimate friend of the Queen and who died in 1822. She is giving an interesting account of an interview between Her Majesty, the Count de Maurepas, herself and St.-Germain. The last-named had paid Mme. D'Adhémar a visit of momentous importance to the Royal family and to France, had departed, and the minister, M. de Maurepas, had come in and was slandering St.-Germain outrageously, calling him a rogue and a charlatan. Just as he had said that he would send him to the Bastille, the door opened and St.-Germain entered, to the consternation of M. de Maurepas and the great surprise of the Countess. Stepping majestically up to the Minister, St.-Germain warned him that he was ruining both monarchy and kingdom by his incapacity and stubborn vanity, and ended with these words: "Expect no homage from posterity, frivolous and incapable Minister! You will be ranked among those who cause the ruin of empires." . . . "M. de Saint-Germain, having spoken thus without taking breath, turned towards the door again, shut it and disappeared . . . all efforts to find the Count failed." Compare this with the several disappearances of H.P.B. in and near Karli Caves and elsewhere, and see how the two agents of the Brotherhood employed identical means for making themselves invisible at the critical moment.

He kept house sumptuously and accepted invitations to dinner from kings and other important persons, but always with the understanding that he should not be expected to eat or drink with the company; and, in fact, he never did, giving as his excuse that he was obliged to follow a special and very strict regimen. It was said that he kept his body strong, young and healthy by taking elixirs and essences, the composition of which he kept secret; it is alleged that his visible diet was only what we might call oatmeal porridge, and that also was prepared by himself. M. Léclaireur says that he "often retired very late, but was never exhausted; he took great precautions against the cold. He often threw himself into a lethargic condition which lasted from thirty to fifty hours, and during which his body seemed as if dead. Then he reawakened, refreshed and rejuvenated and invigorated by this magical repose, and stupefied those present by relating all important things that had passed in the city or in public affairs during the interval. His prophecies as well as his foresight never failed."

This recalls the story told by Collin de Plancy (*Dictionnaire Infernal*, Vol. II, 223) about Pythagoras who, on returning from his journeyings on the astral plane "knew perfectly all that had happened on earth during his absence".

To continue our comparison of the two "messengers," friends and co-workers, we see that H. P. B. did not confine herself to porridge or even a non-flesh diet, but, like the Count, she too would fall into these states of lethargy when she was oblivious to surrounding things, but would come back full of her experiences during the interval of her temporary physical abstraction. In the first Vol. of *O. D. L.* these "brown study" states are described, as also the changes in her moods and manners as one Master after another came "on guard". It is also recorded how the new entity coming in had to pick up out of the brain of the body the register of what had just been transpiring; sometimes making palpable mistakes. Unfortunately we have no record of the effect produced on St.-Germain by suddenly awakening him out of this recuperative trance condition, probably because he always took precautions against such a thing happening; but in the case of H. P. B. I have described the great shock that she experienced when suddenly and unexpectedly dragged back into physical consciousness; more than once she held my hand against her heart to let me feel it beating like a trip-hammer, and she told me that, under certain circumstances, such a thing might be fatal. I am not alluding to those cases where she would leave her body for one or more hours to be worked by one or other of the Masters who were superintending the production of *Isis Unveiled,* but only to those brief withdrawals from the external to the internal plane of consciousness.

In another point there was a great difference between the two messengers. St.-Germain would, very often, when the conversation turned upon any given epoch of the past, describe what had happened as though he had been present, and, as

Baron Gleichen tells us, "would depict the most trifling circumstances, the manners and gestures of the speakers, even the room and the place in it they had occupied, with a detail and vivacity which made one think that one was listening to a man who had really been present. . . He knew, in general, history minutely, and drew up mental pictures and scenes so naturally represented, that never had any eye-witness spoken of a recent adventure as did he of those of the past centuries." The revelations of psychometry have made it perfectly easy for us to understand how a man of St.-Germain's evident adeptship could recall out of the "galleries of the astral light the incidents of any given historical epoch, even to the details of house construction, furnishing and decoration, and the appearance, actions, speech and gestures of the inhabitants; and by spreading out his observations like a spider's web in different directions, get at any facts that he might wish to cite in the conversation then going on. Without having been incarnate at that remote time, he would thus make himself in very truth an eye-and ear-witness of the period in question." Such is the splendid potentiality of Buchanan's epoch-making discovery. Do we not find in Denton's *Soul of Things* scores of cases where trained *psychometers* did this very thing? And if the members of Denton's family could do so much without previous occult training, why should not so grandiose a being as St.-Germain have been able to do much more?

We have seen above that he persistently mystified those inquisitive persons of all ranks—royal, noble and plebeian—who tried to penetrate the secret of his birth, country and age. Have we not also seen H.P.B. playing the same trick on her troublesome inquisitors? Sometimes she would say that she was eighty years old, sometimes that she was born in the eighteenth century, and we have on record the testimony of a newspaper correspondent who, after watching her throughout the evening, said and wrote that she seemed at one moment an old woman and at the next a young girl, while more than one person saw her physical appearance change from one to the other sex. Then we have the case where, when she and I were alone in the room of our "Lamasery" at New York, she attracted my attention and I saw rise out of her body that of a Master with his Indian complexion and black hair, thus for the moment extinguishing the woman of Caucasian type, blue eyes and light hair, who sat before me.

Léclaireur says, in proof of the Count's prodigious memory, that "he could repeat exactly and word for word the contents of a newspaper which he had skimmed over several days before; he could write with both hands at once; with the right a poem, with the left a diplomatic paper, often of the greatest importance. Many living witnesses could, at the beginning of this century (18th), corroborate these marvellous faculties. He read, without opening them, closed letters, and even before they had been handed him." Here, again, we are made to recall the feats of the same sort which H.P.B. did in the presence of witnesses, myself included. She, too, would not only read closed letters before touching them, but also pick up a pencil and write their contents, as in the cases of Mr. Massey and others at New York, and that of the Australian Professor Smith at Bombay, which latter was interesting. One morning Damodar received four letters by one post, which contained Mahāṭmic writing, as we found on opening them. They were from four widely separated places and all post-marked. I handed the whole mail to Prof. Smith, with the remark that we often found such writings inside our mail correspondence, and asked him first to kindly examine each cover to see whether there were any signs of its having been tampered with. On his returning them to me with the statement that all were perfectly satisfactory, so far as could be seen, I asked H. P. B. to lay them against her forehead and see if she could find any Mahāṭmic message in either of them. She did so with the first few that came to hand, and said that in two there was such writing. She then read the messages clairvoyantly and I requested Prof. Smith to open them himself. After again closely scrutinising them, he cut open the covers, and we all saw and read the messages exactly as H. P. B. had deciphered them by clairvoyant sight.

A form of phenomenon, however, which we do not find recorded of St.-Germain, was that of the interception of letters in the post, which in my opinion is among the most remarkable things that I ever witnessed. The whole story is told in *O. D. L.*, First Series, pp. 35, 36, 37, but it may be summarised in a few words. I had come over from New York to Philadelphia on a visit to H. P. B., as I was giving myself a short rest after seeing Eddy's book, *People from the Other World*, out of the press. Intending to stay only two or three days, and not knowing what my Philadelphia address would be, I had left no instructions for the forwarding of my postal matter; but finding that she insisted on my making a longer visit, I went to the Philadelphia Post Office, gave the address of her house and asked that if anything came for me, it should be sent there. I was expecting nothing, but somehow or other I was impelled to do as I did. That very afternoon, letters from South America, Europe and some of the Western States of the Union were delivered at the house by the postman, H.P.B.'s house address being written in lead pencil on each cover. But, and this is what gives the stamp of evidential value to the phenomenon, the New York address was not crossed off, nor did the post-mark of the New York Post Office appear on the backs of the covers, as proof that they had reached the destination intended by my several correspondents. Anybody with the least knowledge of postal matters will see the great importance of these details. Now, on opening the letters which came to me in this fashion during my fortnight's visit to my colleague, I found inside many of them, if not all, *something written in the same handwriting as that in letters I had received in New York from the Masters, the writing having been made either in the margins or any other blank space left by the writers.* The things written were either some comments on the character or motives of the writer, or matters of general purport as regards my occult studies.

The histories of the times all speak of St.-Germain and of the important part played by him in current politics of more than one reign. Thus he is said to have had much to do with the accession of the Empress Catherine to the throne of Russia. He was the intimate friend of Frederick the Great of Prussia, of Louis XV of France, of the Landgraf von Hessen, and of various princes and other great nobles. For many years he occupied a great place in the public thought of various courts and nations, but, of a sudden, in the year 1783, he disappeared from public view with the same mystery attending his exit from the scene as attended his appearance. We have no record whatever of his fate, beyond the statement of his friend, the Prince of Hesse Cassel, that he died in 1783, while making some chemical experiments at Eckrenford, near Schleswig. There is absolutely no historical record of the last illness or death of this man who, for many years, agitated the courts of Europe, nor one word about the disposal of the alleged colossal fortune, in gems and gold, that he had always with him. As Léclaireur says: "A man who had so brilliant a career cannot be extinguished so suddenly as to fall into oblivion."

Moreover, as the same author says: "It is reported that he had a very important interview with the Empress of Russia in 1785 or 1786. It is related that he appeared to the Princess de Lamballe when she was before the revolutionary tribunal, shortly before they cut off her head, and to the mistress of Louis XV, Jeanne Dubarry, while she also was awaiting the fatal stroke, in 1793. The Countess d'Adhémar, who died in 1822, left a manuscript note, of date May 12th, 1821, and fastened with a pin to the original MS., in which she says that she saw M. de Saint-Germain several times after 1793, *viz.*, at the assassination of the Queen (Oct. 16th, 1793); the 18th Brumaire (Nov. 9th, 1799); the day following the death of the Duke d'Enghien (1804); in the month of January, 1813; and on the eve of the murder of the Duke de Berri (1820). "It is to be observed in this connection that these later visits to his friend, the Countess, after his disappearance from Hesse Cassel and his supposed death, may have been made in the same way as that of a Master to myself at New York—in the projected astral body; for we have, in Mrs. Cooper-Oakley's article, a quotation from Grafer's "Memoirs," the statement that St.-Germain told him and Baron Linden that he should disappear from Europe at about the end of the 18th century, and betake himself to the region of the Himalayas, adding: "I will rest; I must rest. Exactly in eighty-five years will people again set eyes on me. Farewell, I love you." The date of this interview may be deduced approximately from another article in the same volume, where it is said: "St.-Germain was in the year 1788, or 1789, or 1790, in Vienna, where we had the never-to-be-forgotten honour of meeting him." If we take the first date, then eighty-five years would bring us to 1873, when H. P. B. came to New York to find me; if the second, then the eighty-five years would coincide with our meeting at Chittenden; if the third, that marks the date of the foundation of the Theosophical Society and the commencement of the writing of *Isis Unveiled,* in which work, as above stated, I am persuaded that St.-Germain was one of the collaborators.

I have thus very briefly, yet in good faith, traced the connection between those two mysterious personages, St.-Germain and H. P. Blavatsky, messengers and agents of the White Lodge, as I believe. The one was sent to help in directing the convergent lines of karma that were to bring abont the political cataclysm of the 18th century with all its appalling consequences, to let loose the moral cyclone which was to purify the social atmosphere of the world; the other came at a time when materialism was to meet its Waterloo and the new reign of spiritual high-thinking was to be ushered in through the agency of our Society.

Printer: G. Subbayya Chetty, Vasanta Press, Adyar

ADYAR PAMPHLETS

No. 91

Yoga-Practice in the Roman Catholic Church

BY

FRANZ HARTMANN

July 1918

THEOSOPHICAL PUBLISHING HOUSE

ADYAR, MADRAS, INDIA

Yoga-Practice in the Roman Catholic Church[1]

THE SPIRITUAL EXERCISES OF IGNATIUS DE LOYOLA

(Founder of the Order of Jesuits)

THE study of comparative religion being one of the objects of the Theosophical Society, it may be of some interest to compare the yoga-practices of the Roman Catholic Church with those described in the Oriental writings. We will then find that they are to a certain extent identical, consisting principally in meditation (prayer), shakṭi, self-control, abnegation, faith, concentration, contemplation, etc., or what Shaṅkarāchārya describes as Shama, Ḍama, Uparaṭi, Ṭiṭīkṣha, Shraḍḍha and Samāḍhana, not to forget bodily posture and the regulation of breath (Prāṇāyāma).

The most detailed instructions are contained in the writings of Ignatius de Loyola, a Catholic Saint, and founder of the (later on ill-reputed) Order of Jesuits. He was an officer in the Spanish army, born at Guipozcod in 1491, as the son of a nobleman. After

[1] Reprinted from *The Theosophist*, February, 1911.

having been severely wounded in battle, his mind took a religious turn; he abandoned his military career, became an ascetic, made a pilgrimage to Jerusalem, studied afterwards at Salamanca and Paris, and became in 1541 General of the Order of Jesuits. His writings have been translated into German by B. Kohler, and the following pages contain some extracts from the same.

The exercises prescribed by Loyola are calculated to develop the powers of the soul, especially imagination and will. The disciple has to concentrate his mind upon the accounts given in the Bible of the birth, suffering and death of Jesus of Nazareth, as if these were actual historical facts. He thus regards them, as it were, as a mental spectator, but by gradually working upon his imagination he becomes, so to say, a participator of it; his feelings and emotions are raised up to a state of higher vibrations; he becomes himself the actor in the play, experiences himself the joys and sufferings of Christ, as if he were the Christ Himself; and this identification with the Object of his imagination may be carried on to such an extent that even stigmata, or bleeding wounds corresponding to those on the body of the crucified Christ, will appear on his body. In this way compassion and love are awakened and developed within the soul, and as the love of a divine ideal is something quite independent of the correctness of the scientific opinion which we may have concerning the actual existence of that ideal itself, this way of awakening divine love by the power of imagination may be very well suited for those for whom love without an object is at first unattainable. Therefore the spiritual exercises of Loyola consist principally of regularly prescribed and gradually ordered meditations and contemplations of the passion of Christ. If properly executed, they may produce freedom from the illusion of self and awaken the power of discrimination (Viveka) between the eternal ego and the temporal self.

The exercises and penances which Loyola taught to his disciples he practised himself, and they were by no means easy. He spent seven hours in prayer, and scourged himself three times every night for the purpose of subduing the desires of his "flesh". Some of the Catholic Orders still practise such severe exercises. The Trappists, for instance, have to work very hard, and their only recreation is prayer. Each brother receives at his entrance to the Order a gown as his only garment, which he has to wear until the hour of his death, without ever being permitted to take it off, whether in daytime or at night, unless it should become so dilapidated as to have to be replaced by a more solid one. Their Matins begin at midnight, lasting for one hour, and one being followed at short intervals by others, so as to allow very little time for rest. They are exposed to the summer heat and have to do without fire in winter, being permitted only a hard bed to sleep on and barely sufficient cover. Moreover they are not permitted to speak with each other or with anybody, and the food they receive is hardly sufficient to keep up their strength.

The Catholic Church, as a whole, may be regarded an as *exoteric* school of religion, and the different Orders therein as *esoteric* schools for practising Yoga. How far some of these Orders have become degraded and have lost the right to be called schools for Yoga, is not our purpose to investigate at present. Certain, however, it is that the Mysteries contained in the Catholic Church are far too high to be grasped by everybody, be he priest or layman, and that the greatest danger which threatens the Catholic Church is the great number of its followers who are incapable of understanding its true spirit, in consequence of which its doctrines are misrepresented and misunderstood. Nevertheless, in some of the Orders practising the above-described austerities, some of these Mysteries are still alive. These people lead a life of great hardship, and there are probably only few among "our parlour-yogīs" and would-be magicians willing to exchange places with them; but we meet smiling faces and joyous hearts among them, and the fact of their having voluntarily taken upon themselves "the Cross of Christ" testifies to their intrepidity and sincerity.

Loyola objects to theoretical explanations regarding the divine Mysteries, as they would only gratify scientific curiosity in unripe minds and disturb them; he only gives instructions concerning the practice of meditation, etc., because, if this practice is properly carried on, the Mysteries will reveal themselves in the natural course of time.

The states of mind under consideration are in their progressive order as follows:

I. *Cogitation.* The state in which the mind is moved and swayed by influences coming from without. These emotions have to be subdued.

2. *Concentration.* The ego assumes power over the thinking process, regulates his thoughts according to his will, and uses them accordingly.

3. *Meditation.* The ego closely examines the object upon which his mind is concentrated.

4. *Contemplation.* The mind enters the object of its meditation; it becomes an indweller of its sphere.

5. *Sanctification.* The mind becomes pervaded and sanctified by this association with the holy object; it becomes penetrated by its divine influence.

6. *Unification.* The contemplating mind becomes one with the object of its contemplation. To this may be added:

7. *Mortification,* or the entire disappearance of the illusion of separateness; there is no separate self which knows, because the knower, the known and the knowledge are one.

The object of meditation is, as has already been stated, the life and suffering of Christ. This is divided into different periods for contemplation, from the Incarnation to the Crucifixion and Resurrection. At first only the memory is called into action by studying the supposed historical facts; next comes the imagination, associating itself with the actors in the divine play, and finally the mind becomes the actor itself;

i.e., Christ is born, lives, becomes crucified and resurrected within ourselves.

There are numerous instructions given as to how these practical exercises are to be carried out, of which we will mention the following:

The first thing is to free oneself from all sinful thoughts and sensual emotions, and to seek to realise the direct action of the divine will; one should not seek to pry with one's intellect into the divine Mysteries, but wait in humility for their interior revelation. This is far more useful in the end than lengthy explanations on the part of the teacher.

The disciple should, while engaged with one object of meditation during one week, not be informed of what will be the object given to him for the next period; but he should be warned against the aggressions of evil spirits, and have their nature explained to him.

He should meditate for five hours every day, beginning at midnight, each meditation lasting at least one hour, and he must not let his mind wander from the object of his meditation.

He should never make a solemn promise or vow until he is perfectly certain that he is able to keep it; that is to say, until God (the Master) Himself reveals to the soul His readiness to receive her. Then he does not follow his own selfish desires, but obeys the divine will.

The teacher should not seek to pry into the sins and innermost thoughts of the disciple; nevertheless he should observe him, so as to be able to give him such guidance and instruction as his case may require.

Ignorant and uneducated persons cannot be guided in the same manner as those who have more intelligence. No one should be offered spiritual truths which he is not yet ripe enough to grasp or comprehend.

Each meditation should begin with prescribed prayers (the "Lord's Prayer," "*Ave Maria*," etc.).

The candidate should go to confession once in every week, and take every fourteen days the holy sacrament of communion.

He should separate himself from all his friends and acquaintances, and avoid all external disturbances, directing his mind solely to the service of God. The more he frees himself from all external attractions, the more will he become ready to receive the light, the grace, and the blessing of God.

The disciple should be instructed, according to the degree of his capacity to understand, about the origin and the real object of his life, which is to praise God and to serve Him. He ought to be made to see the relative worthlessness of all earthly things, and the value of that which is of eternal duration.

He should examine himself carefully every day, and compare the results of each examination with those of the previous one, in the same way as a father watches his child to see what progress it makes.

He should carefully avoid all doubt and despair and also all spiritual pride, and not dwell upon his own personal merits, but sacrifice them to God.

Special Directions

Upon rising in the morning the disciple should at once firmly resolve to avoid all those sins of which he wishes to purify himself, and hold fast to that resolution during the day. Before retiring to rest he should examine himself again, to see whether he has been steadfast in his purpose, and it is useful to note his failures in some diary.

Resist and suppress every evil thought as soon as it arises.

Avoid all useless talk and gossip.

Look upon all wordly possessions with contempt; desire nothing for yourself, neither bodily comfort nor mental consolation, neither riches nor fame.

The disciple should be indifferent to wealth or poverty, honour or disgrace, suffering and death, and always be ready joyfully to accept martyrdom for the glorification of Christ.

Here follow certain rules which may be found somewhat objectionable from our point of view, namely:

He should never think of agreeable things, such as the joys of Paradise, but always have his mind dwelling upon grief and repentance for his sins, and think of death and the Last Judgment.

He should always keep his room dark and exclude all light, keeping doors and windows closed, except while he is praying, reading or eating.

He ought never to laugh, nor say aught that may cause hilarity in others.

He ought never to look at anyone, except at receiving and taking leave of a visitor.

He ought to avoid in eating or sleeping not only that which is superfluous, but even as much as possible of what is considered necessary.

He ought to castigate and lacerate his body by means of lashes, applied with rods or ropes or in other ways, but without injuring the bones. This is for the purpose of doing penance for past sins and for conquering the lusts of the flesh, and also for entering into sympathy with the tortures suffered by our Lord Jesus Christ.[1]

The Three Methods of Prayer

The first method or step is to meditate successfully upon the seven mortal sins, the three powers of the soul, and the five senses of the body. This may be done while standing, sitting, kneeling, or in a recumbent position. While meditating upon the seven deadly sins, compare them with the seven cardinal virtues.

The second step is to meditate about the meaning of each separate word of the prayer, sitting or kneeling, and keeping the eyes either closed or gazing steadfastly upon some selected spot, and not letting his thoughts or eyes wander around.[2]

[1] It is hardly necessary to remark that these ascetic exercises have fallen generally out of use, and are only practised by certain religious Orders at certain times, or by some especially fanatical persons.

[2] Compare *Bhagavad-Gītā*, VI, 13.

Thus he ought to remain for one hour or more, always beginning his meditation with an invocation, and ending with repeating the "Lord's Prayer," "*Credo*," "*Anima-Christi*" and "*Salve Regina*". He ought not to proceed to meditate about another word before he has found in the previous one full satisfaction.

The third method consists in regulating the breath according to a certain measure of time. While drawing each breath some word of the prayer ought to be spoken within the heart, so that between each inhalation and exhalation, and during the whole time that this lasts, only one word is inwardly spoken. For instance, if you meditate about the "Lord's Prayer," beginning with "Our Father, which art in heaven," let your whole attention be directed only to the word "our" and its meaning, and then proceed to the next word, etc.

The Mysteries of the Life of our Lord Jesus Christ

These Mysteries cannot be satisfactorily explained to the human intellect; but they can be spiritually grasped by identifying oneself with the events historically described in the *New Testament*, and mentally participating therein.

In this way the imagination acts upon the will and the emotional nature, causing the higher vibrations of the soul to enter into action, to lift the mind up to the region of spiritual perception, and the love of God to enter the heart. It is then necessary to learn to discern between good and evil influence. Only God has the power to illuminate the mind without any preceding cause; but if there is such a cause, the good angels, as well as the evil ones, may send comfort to the soul; the first ones with good intentions, the evil ones with an evil object (such as to incite vanity or spiritual pride, etc.) in view, and the evil spirit may assume the shape of a messenger of light for the purpose of leading us to perdition. We therefore ought to examine the origin, current, and object of our thoughts. If the beginning, the middle and the end are good and the object the highest, it is the sign of a good influence; but if the thoughts are disturbed by doubts and turned to inferior objects, it is a sign that an evil spirit is at their back. Moreover the touch of a good influence is mild and sweet, and that of an evil one at first harsh and disturbing; but if the heart is inclined to evil, the evil spirit also enters silently, as if it were into his own house through the open door.

Finally it may be of some interest to hear what Loyola says in regard to the Church:

> We must never use any judgment of our own, but be always ready to obey in all things the orders of the true bride of Christ, our holy mother, the Church.
>
> If I see that a thing is white and the Church calls it black, I have to believe in its being black.
>
> We must always approve of and praise the sayings and doings and manners of our superiors, whatever they may be; even if they are not such as can be praised

publicly, because to do so would lower these persons in the estimation of the crowd.

One ought not, to the ignorant, to say much about "predestination" (Karma); because, instead of working for their own improvement, they will become lazy and say: "Why should I trouble myself?—If it is my predestination to be saved, I will be all right, and if I am predestined to be damned, I cannot prevent my damnation." One ought also not to speak about the divine grace of God as if it were a gift, rendering all our own works unnecessary. The highest truths are frequently misunderstood, and the best medicine becomes a poison if misapplied.

Some of the rules given by S. Ignatius de Loyola may be objectionable, but nowhere do we find among them the often quoted Jesuitical maxim that the object sanctifies the means. Moreover there is no doubt that while an object, be it holy or unholy, cannot sanctify its means, a holy purpose can and will sanctify the means, provided they are neither holy nor unholy, but indifferent. Thus for instance, the using of a knife upon a man's body may be a holy or unholy act. If it is done for the purpose of cutting his throat, it is unholy; but if the surgeon uses it for saving a person's life it is holy, and the purpose sanctifies the means.

The Roman Catholic Church has originally derived its doctrines and practices, and even its ceremonies, from the Northern Buddhistic School. Loyola is a true representative of its spirit. His spiritual exercises are in many ways identical with the instructions given in the East for the practice of Raja-Yoga, and a comparison of the two systems may be useful for those who do not merely desire to gratify their curiosity in regard to the astral plane, but desire to become more spiritual by letting the divine powers within their soul become awakened and developed through the influence of divine Love, divine Wisdom, and eternal Life.

Printer: G. Subbayya Chetty, Vasanta Press, Adyar.

ADYAR PAMPHLETS

No. 92

The Soul as It is and How to Deal with It

BY

PROFESSOR GILBERT MURRAY

August 1918

THEOSOPHICAL PUBLISHING HOUSE

ADYAR, MADRAS, INDIA

By kind permission of Professor Gilbert Murray we include this article in our ADYAR PAMPHLETS Series.

The Soul as It is, and How to Deal with It[1]

I

In Tolstoy's novel, *The Cossacks*, there is a scene where a man swimming is shot dead and drifts to the shore, while his slayer swims over the flooded river to get him and crouches down exhausted at his side. There the two lie, looking almost the same. But one is full of a turmoil of desires and aspirations, mingled feelings of pride and misery; and the other is dead. And the only sign of difference is a light steam rising from the body of the living man.

So small a sign, and yet all the difference that can be!

A distinguished anthropologist, Dr. Elliot Smith, has suggested to us the kind of speculation that would go on in the mind of a primitive man if he found a dead body preserved, as it might be, for instance, in the dry Egyptian sand—the phenomenon that led up to the practice of embalmment. What is wrong with that body in the sand? What is it that it lacks?

[1] Reprinted from the *Hibbert Journal*, January, 1918.

It does not breathe. There is no breath in it; that is the first thing that strikes our Egyptian; so he gives it breath as best he can, burning incense under its nostrils, so that the breath may enter in, warm like the breath of the living, and fragrant to correct the smell of the corpse. Again, it is all dry, there is no blood in it: and our Egyptian knows that the blood is the life, because he has seen wounded men die as their blood ebbed away. So he pours libations of blood into the grave, that the dead may get their life again. Some of us will remember the weird passage in *Odyssey*, xi, where Odysseus sees the ghosts of the departed, like puffs of wind made visible, as it were; *psuche kai eidolon*, "a breath and an image," and no more; with no life nor power of thought till they have drunk the blood that he has poured out for them.

If you start thus from the dead body, it seems as if the life or soul lay in some breath or spirit that has departed. Most of our words for the soul show that origin. The word "soul" itself is of doubtful derivation; but "ghost" means "breath," "spirit" means breath. In Latin *spiritus* and *animus* and *anima* are simply breath or wind; in Greek *psuche* is wind, and *pneuma* breath, and *thumos* smoke or vapour. All the words are metaphors; naturally and inevitably so. For whenever mankind notices a new fact and wants to find a name for it, he must needs search about for something like it among the facts he already knows and has names for. The new fact does not come with a name ready written upon it.

The word "life," oddly enough, means "body". I think that comes from another line of thought, in which mankind, when trying to express the thing we call soul or life, started not from the dead body but from a dream-image or phantom. A dream-image, a shape seen in hallucination, a reflection in water or a looking-glass: what is wrong with them, and how are they lacking in the life of the living? Why, they are like those ghosts in Homer. There is "a breath and an image," but no heart or blood or solidity. They are not real. If they could drink of blood and grow solid, if they could get themselves a body, that would be life.

Another mode of thought which started from the dream-image conceived that that image itself was the soul or life; that it moved out of the body in sleep, and sometimes in waking time; moved out and drifted far away at its will and pleasure, with always the possible danger of losing its way and not being able to return to the body. That mode of thought explains the curious pictures in ancient times of the soul as a little human being, sometimes with wings and sometimes without, who lives inside the ordinary body and keeps it alive. There is a common phrase in Homer describing death: "the life left the bones." The word for life there is *thumos*, the word that means smoke or vapour; but the old vase-paintings which depict that kind of death show not a smoke but a beautiful little winged human figure springing out from the body as it falls, and rising heavenward.

II

What does all this amount to? What conclusion can we draw from these stumbling efforts of instinctive man to describe or name or depict this thing within us, which no man has ever seen or heard or touched, and yet which makes the greatest of all differences, the difference between the living and the dead?

I think we can conclude just thus much, that there is something really there, and that man's powers of thought and language, trained as they are on the experience of the material world, have been unable to define or comprehend it. Our modern phraseology is practically all derived from the Greeks, and the Greeks went on using metaphors to the end. If the indescribable thing was not a breath or a wind, then it was a spark of fire; but not ordinary fire, which destroys and perishes; rather the celestial fire of which the stars are made, the stars which neither consume nor are consumed. Or is it a fragment, as it were, of God Himself prisoned in our earthly material, imperfect because fragmentary, yet in some way akin to the Most High? No need to trouble with further attempts at such description; the main result that remains from these broken speculations, on which the world has been living ever since, is the profound conviction of Greek philosophy that man, in some unexplained way, consists of two parts, of which one is living and one dead. "What art thou?" said the Emperor Marcus

Aurelius to himself. "*A little soul carrying a corpse.*"

Plato, the earliest author who discusses and supports with argument the great doctrine that the soul is immortal—that the soul is life, and therefore cannot die—is fond of metaphors about the soul. He is unconsciously founding a new science, that "science of the soul" which we call psychology. His first division of the soul is a very fruitful and interesting one. How is it that the soul shows itself in action? In other words, how is it that a man shows he is really alive? There are three ways, says Plato, desire, and anger and reason; or—since it is hard to get words simple and large enough to express the Greek, by lusting, fighting and thinking. There are things it craves for, and things it hates and rejects; but above the craving and rejecting there is a power of judging, of distinguishing between good and evil and shaping its own course. This power, which he calls reason and we moderns mostly call "will," is the very soul itself. The lusting and fighting, though they may serve the soul, and are forms of life, are mere functions of the live body. A man's soul, he says in another fine passage, is like a charioteer upon a chariot with two horses. One of the horses is sluggish, lazy, tending always downward; the other fierce, but of generous nature and full of courage; and the man who drives them has to master the two of them, keep them abreast, and above all choose for himself the path he means them to take. The charioteer is the real soul.

"*A little soul carrying a corpse*": what is there wrong about that description, or rather, what would be wrong with it if it were ever meant to be literally and exactly true? It is that it separates the body and soul too sharply. That is the mistake in all these primitive conceptions with which we have been dealing, and consequently in a great deal of our own current language, which of course is descended, as all language is, from the philosophy of earlier times. If you have a lump of hot iron, the thought of primitive man will probably regard it as made up of two separate things, heat and a lump of iron. Just as we have certain pictures by savages—and I believe also by children—in which an angry man is shown by drawing first a man, and second his anger, seated inside him or sticking out of his head. Just as in primitive poetry, a man constantly holds conversations with his own heart or his own thought, as if it was a separate thing. It was another Greek philosopher, Aristotle, who cleared that matter up. You meet angry men, not first anger and then men; you meet live persons, not first a life or soul and then a body which it is carrying about. But with that passing caution against possible misunderstanding we shall find it simpler to use the ordinary language, and speak as if the body and the breath or soul inside it were entirely different things.

"A little soul carrying a corpse": the modern writer who has made that old Stoic phrase most clear to the average reader is, I think, M. Bergson. To him man consists of a body which is so much matter, governed by the law of gravitation and all the other laws of dead matter, governed also by the laws of biology or animate matter; and a soul or will—Plato's charioteer—which is free and moves of itself. How the will can be free, of course, is one of those problems which no one can satisfactorily explain. It seems impossible to understand how it can be free; yet almost more impossible to imagine that it is not free. It is an old problem, perhaps an eternal one. But M. Bergson's special contribution to it, if I understand him aright, is this.

The body is of course subject to mechanical and biological law. Throw it up in the air, it will fall down again. Hit it hard enough, it will break. Starve it, and it will suffer and die. And the exact strain necessary in each case can, within limits, be calculated. Furthermore, for much the greater part of life the will—that is, the man himself—acts automatically, like a machine. He is given bad coffee for breakfast, and he gets cross. He sees his omnibus just going, and he runs. He sees in one advertisement that X's boot polish is the best, and on another that Y's boot polish is the best, and he accepts both statements. He does not criticise or assert himself. He follows steadily the line of least resistance. The charioteer is asleep, and the two horses jog along without waking him.

But, says M. Bergson, you will sometimes find that when you expect him to follow the line of least resistance he just does not. The charioteer awakes.

He can resist, he can choose; he is after all a live and free thing in the midst of a dead world, capable of acting against the pressure of matter, against pain, and against his own desires.

Whether this doctrine is exactly true or not, I do not pretend to judge; but it certainly is fruitful. It is just what one feels in one's ordinary experience: a constant tendency to behave like dead matter, to fall into habits, to become by slow degrees—as the ancients put it—" a chained slave ". You are chained by your own standard of comfort; by your conception of what is necessary for you; by your meal-times and the conventions you live among; by the things that you always say or always do or always have. Bergson has for middle-aged men added a new terror to life. He makes you watch yourself becoming mechanical; moving in conformity to outside stimulus; growing more and more dependent on your surroundings—as if the little soul carrying the corpse had found it too heavy and was letting it lie, or perhaps, roll while the soul itself fell half asleep. Fortunately from time to time it wakes, and when it does wake its strength is amazing. A friend of mine wrote to me from amid the heaviest fighting on the Somme, describing the strange impression he received from that awful experience of the utter difference between man's soul and body; the body is so weak and frail a stuff, so easily broken, scattered, torn to rags, or trodden indistinguishably into mire; and the soul so resolute, so untouched and unconquerable.

III

Untouched and unconquerable: those, I think, were my friend's words, and that was the impression which he received. There German shells and bombs and bullets tore men's bodies to pieces without any trouble, but they could not touch the men's souls or change their will. I do not wonder that he received that impression. Yet, is the impression absolutely true? Can we really, without qualification, believe the common, comfortable doctrine that persecution always fails, that the blood of martyrs is always the seed of the Church, that the soul is really unconquerable? The average man does not believe it, much less the ordinary tyrant. In every country he treats such doctrines as mere sentiment, and is perfectly confident that if you give him a free hand with rifle, bayonet, and cat-o'-nine-tails he can stamp out any inconvenient doctrine which puts its trust in nothing more substantial than the soul of man. And I fear the tyrant is not always wrong. Why are there no Protestants in Spain? Not because of the persuasiveness of Spanish theology, but because the Spanish Inquisition did its work. Why are there no descendants of the Albigenses in France? Because they were massacred.

No. We must not delude ourselves into believing that the path of the human soul or conscience when protesting against the world is a safe path, or a path that must in the end lead to victory. It is neither.

It leads for certain through suffering and humiliation; and it may also, it may ultimately, end in defeat. There is no certainty for the protesting soul anywhere; except the certainty of a great uncertainty, of a great battle of unknown issue, in which the odds are by no means as they appear. The big battalions of the world on one side, and the one little soul or group of souls on the other—they are not so unevenly matched after all. The little soul starts indeed with one great handicap against it—it has first to carry its own corpse, and then fight. But if it can do that, if it can get comparatively free from that burden and those entangling chains, get rid of desire and ambition, and hatred and even anger, and think of nothing but what it wills as right, then it is, I will not say unconquerable, but one of the most formidable fighting forces that exist upon this earth.

The doctrine that the persecutor is always defeated and the martyr always triumphant is, I think, little more than mere comfort-seeking, a bye-form of the common vulgar worship of success. We can give great strings of names belonging to the martyrs who were successful, who, whether living or dead, eventually won their causes, and are honoured with books and statues by a grateful posterity. But what of the martyrs who have failed—who beat against iron bars, and suffered and were conquered, who appealed from unjust judges and found no listeners, who died deserted and disapproved by their own people, and have left behind them no name or memorial? How many Belgians, and Serbs, and Poles, how many brave followers of Liebknecht in Germany itself, have been murdered in silence for obeying their consciences, and their memory perhaps blasted by a false official statement, so that even their example does not live? In ancient Athens there was, beside the ordinary altars of worship, an altar to the Unknown God. There ought to be in our hearts, whenever we think with worship and gratitude of the great men who have been deliverers or helpers of the human race, an altar to the unknown martyrs who have suffered for the right and failed.

IV

But let us stop a moment. When the soul of man thus stands up against the world, is it necessarily always in the right? Because a man holds a belief so firmly that he will submit to prison and death rather than forswear it, does it follow that the belief is true? Obviously not in the least. In every great moral conflict of history you have had martyrs on both sides. Christians and Pagans, Arians and Trinitarians, Catholics and Protestants, have killed each other and died themselves for their respective beliefs, and more particularly for those particular parts of them which most directly contradicted the beliefs of the other side. Martyrs are not always right. Indeed, I am not sure that if you took the whole faith for which a particular martyr suffers—the whole mass of passionate beliefs by which he is really at the time actuated—I am not sure you would not find that martyrs were almost always considerably wrong. A man does not usually reach the point where he is willing to die for a cause without getting his passions strongly interwoven with his beliefs; and when a belief is mixed with passion, as we all know, it is almost certain to deviate from truth. If you ever wish, as we all sometimes do, to punish someone who differs from you, and to go on punishing him till he agrees with you, it is no good arguing that your victim is not a martyr because he is wrong or even wicked in his beliefs; a great many martyrs have been wrong, and their persecutors have always thought them both wrong and wicked. It is still more irrelevant to condemn the martyr for being inconsistent: for two reasons. First, there is no person known to history, neither priest nor philosopher, nor statesman, nor even mathematician, who has yet succeeded in building a complete theory of life which has no inconsistencies in it. The best we can do is to be consistent in some little corner of life, or in dealing with some immediate practical problem. And further, it would be absurd to say that a man must not take any step until he had made sure that the whole of his life was consistent with it. If a man wants to behave in some respect better than he has behaved before, it is practically certain that the new and better part of his life will not be consistent with all the other parts of it which he is not attending to. To reproach such a man for inconsistency is equivalent to asking him to remain always at the lowest level of which he is capable—though as a matter of fact he would not attain consistency even then.

You must not be surprised then at a martyr being wrong, and you must not dream of expecting him to be in all of his beliefs consistent.

What can you expect of him, then? I think all you can expect is sincerity of belief and purity of motive. If he is a fool, if he is prejudiced, if he is muddle-headed, if he is misled, if he is exasperating, even if he has certain grave faults of character in other respects, he can still be a martyr, and be entitled to a martyr's reward. But if he is insincere, if he is lying; if, when professing to suffer for the right and the truth, he is really seeking his own advantage, and saying things which he does not believe, then he is done for; there is nothing more to be said about him; he is not a martyr, but a mere ordinary humbug. And no doubt one of the troubles of a Government which has to deal with people who of set purpose and principle defy a particular law, is to make out which are martyrs and which humbugs. And this is a matter of more consequence than may at first appear. For it is a very dangerous thing to allow people by mere cunning and obstinacy and self-advertisement in breaking the law to rise into public fame and to undermine that fabric of mutual agreement which holds society together; a nation in which any well-organised rebels could safely defy the law would soon almost cease to be a free nation. And, on the other hand, a nation in which the Government seems to be forcing men into sin against their conscience, so that good people instinctively respect the prisoner and condemn the judge, has already ceased to be a free nation. You remember the old words of Gamaliel: "Lest haply ye be found to be fighting against God." It is a serious thing for any organ of material power to be found fighting against the human soul.

V

Let me take a present-day instance of this battle between a soul and a Government, a very curious instance, because it is almost impossible without more knowledge than most people in England possess to say who was wrong and who right.

About the year 1889 a young Indian student, called Mohandar Karamchand Gandhi, came to England to study law. He was rich and clever, of a cultivated family, gentle and modest in his manner. He dressed and behaved like other people. There was nothing particular about him to show that he had already taken a Jain vow to abstain from wine, from flesh, and from sexual intercourse. He took his degrees and became a successful lawyer in Bombay, but he cared more for religion than law. Gradually his asceticism increased. He gave away all his money to good causes except the meagrest allowance. He took vows of poverty. He ceased to practise at the law because his religion—a mysticism which seems to be as closely related to Christianity as it is to any traditional Indian religion—forbade him to take part in a system which tried to do right by violence. When I met him in England, in 1914, he ate, I believe, only rice, and drank only water, and slept on the floor; and his wife, who seemed to be his companion in everything, lived in the same way. His conversation was that of a cultivated and well-read man with a certain indefinable suggestion of saintliness. His patriotism, which is combined with an enthusiastic support of England against Germany, is interwoven with his religion, and aims at the moral regeneration of India on the lines of Indian thought, with no barriers between one Indian and another, and to the exclusion as far as possible of the influence of the West, with its industrial slavery, its material civilisation, its money-worship and its wars. (I am merely stating this view, of course, not either criticising it or suggesting that it is right.)

Oriental peoples, perhaps owing to causes connected with their form of civilisation, are apt to be enormously influenced by great saintliness of character when they see it. Like all great masses of ignorant people, however, they need some very plain and simple test to assure them that their hero is really a saint and not a humbug, and the test they habitually apply is that of self-denial. Take vows of poverty, live on rice and water, and they will listen to your preaching, as several of our missionaries have found; come to them eating and drinking and dressed in expensive European clothes—and they feel differently. It is far from a perfect test, but there is something in it. At any rate I am told that Gandhi's influence in

India is now enormous, almost equal to that of his friend the late Mr. Gokhale.

And now for the battle. In South Africa there are some 150,000 Indians, chiefly in Natal; and the South African Government, feeling that the colour question in its territories was quite sufficiently difficult already, determined to prevent the immigration of any more Indians, and if possible to expel those who were already there. This last could not be done. It violated a treaty; it was opposed by Natal, where much of the industry depended on Indian labour; and it was objected to by the Indian Government and the Home Government. Then began a long struggle. The whites of South Africa determined to make life in South Africa undesirable, if not for all Indians, at least for all Indians above the coolie class. Indians were specially taxed, were made to register in a degrading way; they were classed with negroes, their thumb-prints were taken by the police as if they were criminals. If, owing to the scruples of the Government, the law was in any case too lenient, patriotic mobs undertook to remedy the defect. Quite early in the struggle the Indians in South Africa asked Mr. Gandhi to come and help them. He came as a barrister in 1893; he was forbidden to plead. He proved his right to plead; he won his case against the Asiatic Exclusion Act on grounds of constitutional law, and returned to India. The relief which the Indians had expected was not realised. Gandhi came again in 1895. He was mobbed and nearly killed at Durban. I will not tell in detail how he settled down eventually in South Africa as a leader and counsellor to his people; how he founded a settlement in the country outside Durban, where the workers should live directly on the land, and all be bound by a vow of poverty. For many years he was engaged in constant passive resistance to the Government and constant efforts to raise and ennoble the inward life of the Indian Community. But he was unlike other strikers or resisters in this: that mostly the resister takes advantage of any difficulty of the Government in order to press his claim the harder. Gandhi, when the Government was in any difficulty that he thought serious, always relaxed his resistance and offered his help. In 1899 came the Boer war; Gandhi immediately organised an Indian Red Cross unit. There was a popular movement for refusing it and treating it as seditious. But it was needed. The soldiers wanted it. And it served through the war, and was mentioned in despatches, and thanked publicly for its skilful work and courage under fire. In 1904 there was an outbreak of plague in Johannesburg, and Gandhi had a private hospital opened before the public authorities had begun to act. In 1906 there was a Native rebellion in Natal: Gandhi raised and personally led a corps of stretcher-bearers, whose work seems to have proved particularly dangerous and painful. Gandhi was thanked by the Governor in Natal—and shortly afterwards thrown into jail in Johannesburg. Lastly, in 1913, when he was being repeatedly imprisoned, among criminals of the lowest class, and his followers were in jail to the number of 2,500, in the very midst of the general strike of Indians in the Transvaal and Natal there occurred the sudden and dangerous railway strike which endangered for the time the very existence of organised society in South Africa. From the ordinary agitator's point of view the game was in Gandhi's hands. He had only to strike his hardest. Instead he gave orders for his people to resume work till the Government should be safe again. I cannot say how often he was imprisoned, how often mobbed and assaulted, or what pains were taken to mortify and humiliate him in public. But by 1913 the Indian case had been taken up by Lord Hardinge and the Government of India. An Imperial Commission reported in his favour on most of the points at issue, and an Act was passed according to the Commission's recommendations, entitled the Indian Relief Act.

My sketch is very imperfect; but the story forms an extraordinary illustration of a contest which was won, or practically won, by a policy of doing no wrong, committing no violence, but simply enduring all the punishment the other side could inflict until they became weary and ashamed of punishing. A battle of the unaided human soul against overwhelming material force, and it ends by the units of material force gradually deserting their own banners and coming round to the side of the soul!

Persons in power should be very careful how they deal with a man who cares nothing for sensual pleasure, nothing for riches, nothing for comfort or praise or promotion, but is simply determined to do what he believes to be right. He is a dangerous and uncomfortable enemy—because his body, which you can always conquer, gives you so little purchase upon his soul.

VI

In Gandhi's case the solution of the strife between him and the Government was particularly difficult, because he was not content to be let alone. He thought it his duty, God helping him, to compel a Government backed by the vast majority of the nation to change their policy. And no Government could yield, or ought to yield, to such coercion. The best it could do was probably somewhere near that which, by the advice of General Smuts, it eventually did propose to do: to purge its policy as far as possible of all elements which were not essential to its own conviction and which did particular violence to the convictions of others.

In the next case I wish to lay before you the issue is much simpler. It is the case of the persecution of an Englishman of saintly life, Stephen Hobhouse. I say deliberately of saintly life, and I say no more; not for a moment that his views are right, or his theory of life socially convenient, or his example one that should be followed. As we have noticed before, it often happens that the saints are wrong and the children of this world right; but they are not often right when they begin treating the saints as criminals.

Stephen Hobhouse began life as the son of rich parents; he was a scholar of Eton, afterwards a scholar of Balliol; he won First Class Honours in Moderations, and Second Class Honours in Greats, after which he obtained a post in the Board of Education. He was rich and well connected; he was clever and successful, and had every prospect of a brilliant career. But from early life he had a conscience more exacting than the consciences of most of us. He was religious with a touch of mysticism. He wanted to follow Christ. He eventually formulated the goal at which he aimed as "self-identification with the oppressed". To help the poor and suffering was not enough; he must be one with the poor and suffering. He could not do this as a rich man. So he began by renouncing his position as heir to his father's estate, and stripping himself of the prospect of inherited wealth. He had, I think, already joined the Quakers, and was a regular speaker in their meeting-house. (They have no ordained ministers.) He went with his wife, who shares his religion, to live in a workman's flat in Hoxton, and the two spent all their time in social work—that is, in ministering to the poor and in the effort towards "self-identification with the oppressed". Their life, I need hardly say, was abstemious to the point of asceticism. Let me give one small illustration.

A friend of mine calling on Mrs. Stephen Hobhouse the other day noticed a clothes-line hanging across the room and asked some question about it,

It appeared that when they first moved into the flat, living of course without a servant, Mrs. Hobhouse sent her washing out to a laundry. The work of suddenly living without a servant was, for two delicate people, hard enough. But they noticed that the families living round them did not send their washing out; they did it at home in the living-room. "Self-identification with the oppressed" pointed the road clearly, and they tied the clothes-line across the living-room and did the washing at home.

Stephen Hobhouse had been a Quaker, and a Quaker of the strictest sort, for ten years before 1914. He had had experience of a previous war; for during the war in the Balkans he had resigned his post in the Board of Education, and gone to Constantinople to nurse the refugees of various nations who were lying, largely untended, in the mosques, particularly in the mosque of St. Sophia. Of his work there I know only by hearsay, but the stories of it sound like stories of St. Francis. Creeds and religious organisations clash against one another; but true saintliness, the quality of the soul that has really mastered the corpse it carries, is much the same in all religions, and breaks the barriers of creeds. Stephen's interpreter, a pious Moslem, who was accustomed probably to think of all Christians as dogs, felt the spirit that radiated from this Christian, and the two used to pray together to the same God.

The present war came and was followed by conscription, embodied in an Act which gave complete exemption to those who on conscientious grounds, however mistaken, refused to take part in slaying their fellow-men. If conscription was necessary, as I am inclined to think it was, that was a generous Act, and one worthy of the traditions of English tolerance. It was well known that Stephen Hobhouse, as a strict Quaker, considered it a sin to partake in war, and there was not the smallest glimmer of a doubt to be cast on the sincerity of his objection.

By an act of deliberate and purposeful injustice his tribunal disallowed his conscientious objection and sent him to the army. He did not appeal against the sentence, because many of his friends and fellow-Quakers were already being sent to prison, and "self-identification with the oppressed" forbade his deserting them. He refused to obey military orders. He was court-martialled and sentenced to various military punishments, culminating in 112 days' hard labour. When that was over he was taken out and the order repeated; of course he still disobeyed, and is now undergoing two years' hard labour. The renewed sentences bring with them conditions more severe than those of continuous penal servitude.

And one point more. Every one interested in prison reform knows that one of the most severe strains upon human nature involved in prison life is the eternal silence—one of the most severe and, many people hold, the most corrupting and injurious to mind and character next to solitary confinement itself. In every prison the rule of silence is apt to be somehow evaded. It is a thing which human nature in the long run will not bear, and by hook or by crook, by sundry unedifying artifices, the prisoners do manage to snatch a few words of conversation with one another from day to day. Stephen Hobhouse at first did talk by these secret methods, then he decided that it was wrong. He writes to his wife: "The very night of thy last visit I was smitten with a sense of shame for the habits of concealment verging on deception which this life seems to force on all of us. For a fortnight I wrestled day and night with this feeling. . . . It seemed so hard to give up the only outward ways of expressing love." He confessed to the governor that he had been breaking the rule of silence, and refused to promise to obey it in the future. And the result is that, in order to make sure he does not break that rule, and at the same time to avoid the constant repetition of special punishments, this man is in solitary confinement for the indefinite future.

I believe in this case that the Government has broken the law. I am certain that the original sentence of the tribunal was wrong. But for the moment I am dealing with another aspect of this case. Apart from the rightness or wrongness of the prisoner's views about war, apart from the technical legality or illegality of the Government's action, you have here a deliberate conflict between the massed power of Government and the soul of one righteous man. There are about a thousand men in the same position.

I do not know who will win. I make no prophecy. It is quite easy for a huge engine like the War Office to crush any one man's body, to destroy his reason by perpetual solitude, or put an end to his life. But I do not think that a Government which sets out to prosecute its saints is a wise or a generous Government; I do not think a nation which cannot live in peace with its saints is a very healthy or high-minded nation.

VII

I have not attempted to answer the question with which we started, to define what the soul is or what life is, or where the difference comes between the mere physical life that makes a man move his limbs and desire his food, and the soul itself or central guiding principle, which the ancients called reason and the moderns think of as will. The question is perhaps still beyond human powers of analysis. I have only tried to consider with the help of examples the actual working of the soul in shaping a man's life, and sometimes bringing him into conflict not only with his own apparent interest, but with the general stream of will in the society around him. And I have tried, first, to suggest that a wise ruler will be very circumspect, a conscientious ruler will be very tender, before challenging the lowliest of human souls to battle on the soul's own ground, or setting about the task of compelling the humblest of his subjects by torment and violence to do that which he definitely believes to be wrong. So much for action between man and man. And secondly, within our own hearts, I would say that the main lesson to each man of us is to see that his own soul does not die. It will sometimes stagger under the weight of the corpse it carries; that is inevitable. Only let it not fall into the power of the corpse. The weight of dead matter seems, at times like the present, to increase upon us. Our whole being is dulled. We do more and more things because we are driven, fewer and fewer because we choose them and love them; we cease even to suffer as we should suffer, or to pity as we should pity. In our own great war we tend to forget what we ourselves owe to the higher causes for which our friends have died as martyrs, to forget because the deaths are by now so common and the martyrdom has lasted so long. We tend to shrink from the higher emotions because they are difficult, to sink into the round of lower and more commonplace emotions because they make less disturbance in our daily business. The power of death is abroad over the world. It has taken lives innumerable, and better lives than ours. Let those of us whose bodily life is still spared make sure that the soul within us shall not die.

Printer: G. Subbayya Chetty, Vasanta Press, Adyar.

ADYAR PAMPHLETS

No. 93

The Search for Happiness

BY

ANNIE BESANT

September 1918

THEOSOPHICAL PUBLISHING HOUSE

ADYAR, MADRAS, INDIA

The Search for Happiness[1]

THE one thing in which all sentient creatures agree is that happiness is desirable, and some unconsciously, some deliberately, some under cover of another object placed ostensibly as that which is sought, engage in the continual pursuit of this one end. Everywhere man is in search of happiness; everything, in fact, around us in which sentient life is found, life capable of experiencing pleasure and pain, every such form of life is engaged in the search after happiness. Some people, with a kind of idea, apparently, that to openly seek for happiness is wrong, or in some way unworthy, cover over the fact of the search by putting forward some other end, some other aim, for life. But if we carefully examine their arguments and their conduct we find that while they may put forward what is really a means as the end at which they are aiming, the very way in which they regard that means shows that it is only an intellectual blunder that they are making in thinking that they are really seeking for that, instead of for the end to which it leads. Many of you, for instance, may have a momentary question in the mind, if you have not thought carefully over the subject before, and you

[1] Reprinted from *The Adyar Bulletin*, 1908.

may be inclined to say: "Is it not virtue that we seek for as the end of life, rather than happiness? Do we not put before ourselves as the highest good right living, rather than bliss?" But that question, if the answer to it be analysed, will be found to be based on a misconception of the facts. Why is it that men follow virtue, save that they find in virtue an inner accord with their own being, and know that in that accord is the only means to permanent happiness? Every religion for instance, you will find, speaking of happiness on the other side of death, speaks of that happiness in connection with virtuous living, and regards it as the very crown and result of the virtue. And, truly, in that idea that happiness is the result of virtue, there is no error, for virtue is the means to happiness, the only practical means, because happiness means harmony with the divine nature, means harmony with the divine law in life, and inasmuch as nature is based on the divine existence, inasmuch as that existence manifests by law and not by arbitrary fancy or whim, it is inevitable that following that Will and the gaining of happiness shall be one and the same thing. In a universe of law, happiness must lie in union with the law, and if that law be a law of good, if it be, as it is, an expression of the divine nature, then virtue is the only road to permanent happiness, and the very test of virtuous conduct is whether it does or does not lead ultimately to happiness as its end.

For in truth as we study this question carefully we must recognise, if we be frank with ourselves, that a line of conduct which leads to misery ever-increasing, and which could only have as its end perpetual misery, is always identical with that which is against law, is that which we speak of as fundamentally vicious and not virtuous. All the consent of the world's thinking, which sees in happiness the inevitable result of virtue, is only really the instinctive prompting of man's nature, which, knowing itself divine, knows bliss to be its inevitable heritage. That God is Bliss, Brahman is Bliss, is found in Indian Scripture and in Christian Revelation. Both give the same teaching, that the very being of the divine is fundamentally happiness and not misery, joy and not sadness, bliss, in a world unending, complete and perfect. That which has sometimes veiled the reality of this as the true end of man has been that often in the course of evolution it is necessary to face a passing sorrow for a more permanent happiness, to sacrifice the lower for the higher, the transitory for the enduring; hence virtue, which means ultimately steady and permanent bliss, may sometimes for a time lead us along a path of pain or self-denial. And even then there is an inner joy, deeper than the surface pain, bearing witness to the identity of right and happiness. But that pain and self-denial we face, knowing that they are temporary, whereas the happiness is permanent; and if we find that a passing bliss gives rise to a permanent unhappiness, then at once we stamp that passing bliss as unworthy of our pursuit, and again vindicate that innermost instinct of our nature that the good and the happy are ultimately identical, that sorrow treads on the heels of evil, as the Lord Buḍḍha said, "as the wheels of the cart follow the heels of the ox," that, by the eternal law, that which is right means ultimately that which is bliss, while that which is evil leads as inevitably to misery; man grasps at evil, deluded by the temporary appearance, because he is ignorant instead of wise, because he is blinded by the transitory form, and the reality underneath that form is veiled from him by the lack of insight and of knowledge.

The inner instinct of man, which drives him to seek for happiness, is definitely justified alike by religion and philosophy. I have already said that all the religions of the world speak of happiness as the outcome of right doing, and the philosophies of the world—which put into intellectual form the roads along which man should intelligently travel—those philosophies either definitely, or implicitly, are all put forward as means of escaping misery. Every great school of Indian philosophy, in opening an exposition in which its principles are detailed, begins with a statement that it is the seeking to put an end to pain. That is put forward definitely as the end of the philosophy, and it is justified by the declarations that inasmuch as the supreme is bliss, as the only true wisdom is knowledge, therefore true philosophy must be the knowledge of God, and in that as inevitably is implied happiness, as light in the being of the sun.

This, then, being recognised as true, religiously and philosophically as well as practically, I propose to look with you to-night on the best way of finding happiness, so that if possible each one of us, finding in our hearts that longing, may know along which road it is best to tread in our search. For the sorrow of the world comes from the world's ignorance; the grief of the world comes from the world's delusion. Men follow what they dream will give them happiness, and over and over again it shivers in their grasp the moment they have seized it, so that human life, too often, is a succession of disappointments, and yet the ineradicable thirst for happiness still drives man along the road of this unending quest.

Now in order to know what will be happiness for us, we must know something of our own nature, must realise its wants, its demands, its cravings, and then we shall be able to discover how best those cravings may be satisfied. And in making this search, it would indeed be well if out of the heart of every one of you could drop that ancient superstition which causes so much unhappiness, that there is something more or less wrong in being happy, that there is something more or less to be ashamed of in finding and enjoying happiness, that that old horror of Calvinism is true, that the Divine Being is pleased with sadness rather than with joy, and that He, whose innermost being is Bliss, can in any sense grudge the enjoyment of happiness by His children.

Suppose, then, that we have got rid of this superstition—and I wish it went out of men's hearts as easily as the phrase can be spoken—then, looking at our own nature and its demands, we may hope to waste less time in following mistaken roads. We may hope to utilise life's experience in the best possible way, in the way in which evolution will also best be advanced.

Man's nature, we have often seen, may for practical purposes be looked at as showing itself in four chief ways :

(*a*) We find ourselves with a physical nature surrounded by a physical world, and in this world the vehicle of our consciousness is the physical body, and all the objects which the world presents to us are objects which either attract or repel us, giving us either pleasure or pain.

(*b*) Then we find, looking into our nature still further, emotions, the emotional nature of man. Those have their satisfaction chiefly in the intercourse with human beings around us, in the interchange of life energies with them, the emotions being best satisfied in our intercourse with humanity. But in addition to that, those emotions are also sources of pleasure or of pain in connection with other objects in the world around us which stir them up, give life to them and expand them, or else knock roughly against them, frustrating them, denying them expansion. All the wondrous world that lies in art, in the satisfaction of the sense of beauty, all that which comes to us, from the splendour of the world around us, from landscape, from colour, from light, from sound, in nature—all these are things that give satisfaction to the emotions within us, and they find their gratification in coming into touch with these harmonious vibrations in nature, to which we in turn harmoniously respond in our emotions. So that there is a second side to our nature, either to be satisfied or to be starved, which will have a very definite relation to this search after happiness, and that needs to be understood that it may be wisely guided, intelligently directed.

(*c*) Then we find, on looking into our nature more closely, an intellectual aspect where thought and reason, the joy of research and of knowledge, the delight in the exercise of the intelligence, of the conquest of new thought, lend happiness to life, and form the keenest enjoyments of those who have developed that aspect of their nature.

(*d*) And when these three ways of expressing ourselves are seen and understood—by way of the body, by way of the emotions, and by way of the intelligence—we find that all these may be satisfied, and yet in the innermost depth of our nature there may still be a craving, demanding satisfaction. It is that instinct in man that arises over and over again, reappearing perennially, however often it may be frustrated, or, for a time, submerged, the longing of the human Spirit for the divine Source whence it came, the aspiration for the perfect, the aspiration for the divine, that ineradicable thirst of man for God which nothing can extinguish, which nothing can destroy, which has embodied itself in religion after religion, which finds its satisfaction through superstition, if it cannot find its satisfaction through knowledge, which is enriched by contributions from the intelligence, from the emotions, from everything that is deepest and most essential in our life, the very Self in us, that yearns after the satisfaction of union with the SELF in all; it is the craving of man to find himself in the One as well as in the many, to find that peace which can never be found in the changing conditions around us, the peace, the stability, the permanence, which are only in the Self, the Self which is divine in its origin, and only finds satisfaction in conscious union with the divine. Human restlessness everywhere eloquently speaks of man's lack of final satisfaction until that peace is found, and in the course of evolution, in the course of our growth, we find that everything fails us save that alone, that however long aught else may last, brought from any other source, in the end it breaks into pieces in our hands, and we are left empty where we had dreamed of fullness.

Very great demands, then, arise for satisfaction from human nature. Sometimes these demands conflict the one with the other, and hence the confused thought of man regarding happiness and right. But perfect happiness would satisfy everything which exists in man's complex nature, everything in him which is permanent, which expresses itself in many ways. Passing manifestations—those may perish and leave us unhappy, but that which is fundamental in our nature, that must be satisfied, else happiness cannot be.

Now, if we look at the men around us, the vast majority, whatever may be their theories of life, we see, by observation, they are seeking their objects of happiness on the material plane. I am speaking of a matter of dry fact, which every one of you can verify by observation. Most of those around us seek some satisfaction of the body, however much for a while it may be veiled. Wealth, perhaps, more than any one thing, is sought by men in all ages, under all conditions of civilisation, but wealth is not sought for itself, not even in the cases which show that strange twist in human nature which identifies the means with the end, giving us the phenomenon of the miser, who cares for wealth for itself, as *he* says, and not for the command which it gives over objects that are seen as yielding pleasure. Wealth is followed by people constantly because of the command that it gives over material objects, not for itself but for the power that lies within it—for that reason men are ever seeking after wealth.

Now the question must at once arise, especially for the young who have their lives before them to plan out and to direct: Is it the path of a wise man, looked at intellectually, to turn the chief endeavours of his life, the chief efforts of his intelligence, the chief strain of his powers, to the mere gathering of anything which will only give satisfaction to the most passing part of his nature? Does happiness really lie in multiplying the wants of the body, or in diminishing them? Along the line of luxury, or along the side of frugality? Along the side of increasing the demands of the body, or along the side of narrowing those demands to the greatest possible extent? There is a question worth thinking over at leisure, worth weighing, analysing and answering. For on the answer to that depends practically the guidance of your life; and on the answer of the majority amongst you depends also the future of the nation. This is one of the great problems that lie before every nation at the present time—whether it tends to pursue the path of material luxury, the multiplication of material wants, seeking more and more gratification by the creation of artificial wants, in luxury, in show, in ever-increasing gratification of ever-increasing material demands. Is it along that road that happiness is to be found either for the individual or for the nation?

Other nations in the past have asked that question, and have answered that happiness is to be sought in luxury, in the multiplication of wants and in their gratification; and the end of it, for every such nation, has been death, not life. Look back in history, and you will find that history is strewn with the wrecks of civilisations, and, if you study those civilisations, you will find that they were ever civilisations that sought increasing luxury of the body, increasing sensual gratification, increasing pleasures in connection with the physical, material life. We are beginning to go —nay, we have been going for a considerable time— along this well-trodden path which so many nations have trodden before us, and, by the madness which possesses each nation in turn, as it occupies the stage of the world, we think that while other nations have perished along that road, we and we only shall escape, that though other civilisations have perished by luxury, ours shall not thus perish, that though other civilisations have grown rotten by luxury, ours will remain vigorous and strong; we are blind to the signs of decadence around us, shown in our art, shown in our literature, as well as in the unbridled luxury of the wealthy, in the ever-increasing search for pleasures that perish in the using; our national civilisation is walking along the road on which history has written but a single word and that word an epitaph: "To the memory of a perished nation, the tombstone of a vanished civilisation!"

Why is death written on all those individuals or nations who seek in the life of the body, however refined, happiness which cannot lie there? The reason is not far to seek. The body, first of all, is a thing of habit, and its happiness is measured, not by the pleasures that you give it, but by the cravings that remain unsatisfied. The happiness of the body quickly wears itself out. The body is so much a creature of habit that, when it has enjoyed anything for a short time, that thing loses its power to give pleasure. Who are the people who enjoy wealth? Not those who are born wealthy, nor even those who long have possessed wealth. The pleasures of wealth are really felt by those who have suffered poverty and who have the power of gratifying cravings that have long been demanding satisfaction. But when these are satisfied, when the satisfaction has become habitual, then weariness takes the place of pleasure, and satiety the place of satisfaction. It is a mark of all physical enjoyments that as they are exercised they gradually lose the power to give pleasure, and that, a little later, disgust and weariness succeed. In all cases of physical enjoyment the limit of enjoyment is narrow, and when that limit is overpassed, a stronger and stronger stimulus is needed to give pleasure, and when that stronger and stronger stimulus is supplied, then the organ by which the pleasure is felt wears out by the very exertion of taking it, and so disgust treads on the heels of pleasure and weariness on the heels of enjoyment.

How much better, then, knowing *that* by study, rather to limit the wants of the body than to increase them; for here again habit stands true and firm. Limit the satisfactions of the body, and the body becomes as happy in the midst of the frugal living as it ever was in the midst of luxurious enjoyment, finds itself as contented with simplicity as with luxury, with sufficiency as with superfluity.

I am not speaking of that pain which no human being in a properly organised society should endure, the pain of starvation, of the absolute lack of those necessities of life which preserve the health of the body. Health is necessary to physical happiness, and every man, woman and child should be under conditions where health is possible, where health is attainable, and where only his own fault brings about the misery of bodily disease, of bodily weakness; the present social miseries are inevitable conditions, which will gradually disappear when men have learned that real happiness does not lie in the physical world.

Now that brings me to a point that is of moment to every one of us. All physical things perish in the using, and therefore are sources of combat and struggle. Where a nation is continually seeking enjoyment, it consumes with every hour of pleasure, it destroys with every satisfaction of its craving, and as, in physical nature, you can multiply desires much faster than you can multiply the objects of desire, the inevitable result is that where one class is luxurious another class is deprived of the ordinary comforts of existence, and that where, at one pole, there is an overwealthy and luxurious class, at the other there is the misery of poverty and of disease. That is the mark of physical gratification that we cannot escape. We cannot produce as fast as we are able to consume. There might be enough produced to give to all the satisfaction of reasonable bodily demands, to make all bodies healthy and physically happy; there never can be enough produced by human labour to give ever-increasing luxury to some without contest and misery amongst those who produce for the few. That is the inevitable truth, the non-recognition of which has brought about the perishing of the civilisations of which I spoke; for unbridled luxury on the one side means misery upon the other, and as long as men place their happiness in the enjoyment of things that perish in the using, so long will society be a field of struggle, a field of battle; for each man, fearing his share will be insufficient, strives to take more than he has need of at the moment, in order to provide for the feared necessities of the future. Hence the young man and the young woman who choose wisely will begin by choosing the physically simple, rather than the physically luxurious life, training the body and disciplining it, instead of pampering it and giving it more than it needs. For the body is an admirable servant, but it is an intolerable tyrant as a master, and you may see the picture of what the body becomes, when it is made master instead of servant, if you look at the worn-out sensualist, the worn-out voluptuary. There is the Nemesis of nature for placing happiness in the body that perishes, instead of in those higher regions of human nature which give to man a happiness other than that of the body.

Pass on to the next department of our nature, and see how far happiness may be found in the gratification of the emotions. Here, if the emotions that are gratified are wisely chosen, far more of value will come into the life, far more growth in humanity, far more progress in evolution. Choose wisely the emotions which you gratify, and they will lift you upwards instead of dragging you down. Make as your rule, in choosing the emotions that are to be gratified, that they shall be those that can be gratified without injury to others, those the gratification of which tends to the happiness of all and not to your own alone, which enable you to add more and more to the joy of the world, which culture in you all that is delicate, refined and comparatively permanent, rather than the emotions which will be gratified along the lower lines of human evolution. Remember, especially if you are dealing with the young, that on the tastes that you develop on the emotional side will largely depend the line of evolution along which the soul will pass, the way in which it will climb out of evil and be attracted to the good.

Take a youth entering into life, in whom physical health is strong, where the demands of the body are violent, and see how unwise is the guidance to which he is too often subjected, how unreasonable the demands that too often are made upon him. If we want to help the young amongst us, boys and girls alike, to grow and develop and have happiness in life, we ought to use all the loftier emotions to raise them out of finding enjoyment in the exercise of the lower. If you find a youth inclined to seek pleasure in vicious indulgences, inclined to give way to the cravings of the lower nature, the way to meet him is not by rebuke, not by anger, not by contempt, but by placing within his reach pleasures that refine instead of pleasures that degrade, pleasures that elevate instead of pleasures that lower. You should use all art, all beauty, all that attracts the growing, developing nature, in order to lead him gently along the road where higher and nobler satisfaction may be found; not by insisting on asceticism, but by training in temperance, will you gradually refine the natures that you have to deal with and lift them above the possibility of temptation. The harm that is over and over again done to youthful natures is in insisting on an unwise asceticism, in pressing on them that which does not attract, and denying them everything that does; whereas when you find the nature reaching out, your duty is to try and satisfy it by gratifying the highest demands in it, and so gradually letting the lower ones be starved out; one reason why, so often, the sons and daughters of religious families turn out wilder and worse than the children of men and women of the world is because the nature has been repressed instead of guided, has been frustrated instead of developed, has been taught to look on all joy as more or less evil and dangerous; hence, as the young will at all risks enjoy, pleasure is grasped at without discrimination, and seized without knowledge. The love of joy, the love of beauty, these are the outstretching hands of the soul, groping after the divine Beauty and the divine Bliss. It is ignorance that makes them grasp in the wrong direction. It is ignorance that makes them choose the paths that lead to sorrow. Guide them, but do not deny them happiness. Help them, do not frustrate their longings; and use their love of beauty and joy to lift them some steps along the path of evolution, teaching them to seek their pleasures in the relatively permanent more than in the transitory, in that which spreads happiness around them instead of that which brings sorrow and degradation in its wake.

The emotions, then, wisely dealt with, are part of that side of our nature which may show us the way to happiness. Wisely dealt with, I say, for in this comes the profound lesson, that love, which is the deepest of the emotions, the gratification of which gives the most permanent delights, must be purified from selfishness, and must more and more find its satisfaction in what it gives, rather than in what it takes. For the love that gives lifts us to the spiritual nature, while the love that takes draws us down the ladder of evolution, and man's place in evolution may be judged by that which is the dominant element in his love, the giving or the taking element. All the sorrow of life comes out of the longing to grasp, to take, to monopolise for ourselves. All its joy—and that joy grows with our growing—lies in its giving, lies in its yielding itself, lies in its pouring out itself and finding happiness in the joy which it creates; that is the love which is divine, which lifts us, which is essentially spiritual, and therefore lasting in its nature; you may use your emotions to lead up to that greatest of possessions, a love which, finding bliss in spreading happiness, can never be taken away from us, can never be broken by any change of circumstances or by any shock of grief.

So also as we go on with our study, we find in the gratification of the intellect another of those lines where the search for happiness will bring an ever-growing gratification. Hard sometimes in the early stages, meaning self-denial and pain which is passing, rewarded with how much happiness that is lasting! You will see, if you analyse the line along which we are going, that more and more happiness is secured as the happiness is based on our own character and nature, and not on the things that surround us, that our happiness grows as we find it in the development of the life within us and not in the grasping at the things around us. To put a startling contrast between the man who has chosen the physical and the man who has chosen the emotional and the intellectual: you may take from the one all the circumstances that gave him happiness, and he lies miserable and wretched, because his life was outside him instead of within; whereas the man who has put his happiness in the growth and the purification and development of the emotions and the intellect, he may be stripped of everything and still remain content and happy, for his life is within him, his strength is within him. The more internal the happiness the more lasting it is in its nature.

But that only leads us on to the one final answer, which is to be the crown of human evolution, which is to give the uttermost satisfaction to the whole nature. Man's true happiness ultimately lies beyond even intellect and emotion, beyond all that art and beauty can do for us, beyond all that literature and genius can bestow upon us, great as are those royal gifts from those who illuminate the world. Far beyond those gratifications lie the pleasures of the spiritual nature, that joy of the innermost essence of the Self, that is ever-increasing not diminishing, that grows with exercise instead of lessening. I put on the physical, as the mark of the folly of therein finding happiness, that it perished in the using, was consumed in the enjoying; but with the development of the higher emotions, with the development of the powers of the intelligence, and still more with the unfolding of the spiritual nature, of which these are the reflected aspects, happiness grows and increases with use, and the more we consume the more we have left. That is true of the intellect. It never gives rise to struggle between man and man, when turned towards pure intelligence. There never can be too many works of genius; there never can be too many triumphs of beauty. The more these powers are exercised, the happier is the world by their results. If I learn a thing, I have first the joy of learning, then the joy of extended vision which is the result of that exercise of the intelligence, then the joy of sharing it with all those who are around me; and the more I give the more I have to give; for it is the glory of the intelligence that the more it gives the more it has to share, the more it expends itself the richer it becomes. If I teach you a truth, I am not the poorer, because you have that truth as well as I; nay, I am the richer, not only because my knowledge is yours, but also because, in the sharing, I know the truth better than I knew it before I taught it. In the very teaching comes added vision; in the very sharing comes added knowledge; in the very giving comes increase of the wealth; to spread knowledge blesses those who give it, still more perhaps than the one who receives it; so that in the giving you grow richer, and the joy is ever-increasing instead of lessening by the gift.

Now, as that is realised, and as we realise still further that in the spiritual world all this is a thousandfold increased, then indeed we see the direction in which our thoughts, our efforts, should be turned, if we would have happiness in life. Nothing makes happiness permanent save the unfolding of the spiritual nature within us. Everything else may fail us; this can fail us never. Beauty—that may fail us; we may lose the power to perceive it. Intelligence—that may fail us; ever the grave closes over us, for it cannot express itself here when its physical organ is decayed; but the life of the Spirit is ever-growing, ever-increasing; it knows no limitation, it knows no frustration, it knows no possibility of loss or destruction. As that increases, we find that all that is permanent in the emotions, all that is permanent in the intelligence, is really part of the spiritual life, the reflection of the eternal beauty and knowledge which are of the very essence of happiness. It is as though the divine Father of life coaxed His children along the road of evolution by placing before them the flowers of emotion and the flowers of intelligence, that they may tread the road that leads upwards to the Self. For we find, as we begin to understand, that all that we knew of joy in the emotions was really a reflection from the perfect beauty of the Self; that it was not in its essence fleeting, that it was not in its essence perishable, that it was and is part of the eternal Beauty, part of the eternal Bliss. If we lose here the objects of our emotions, so that life seems withered of its joy, then, as the Spirit unfolds, we find that we are not separated from them, and that the joy of the emotion between us belongs to the lasting element and not to the temporary, that love is spiritual in its essence, not even emotional in its root, and that they come back to us dearer a thousandfold as the spiritual nature unfolds. And if with regard to the intelligence the physical organ weakens, then we find, as the spiritual nature unfolds, that the intelligence can work in other regions, can work in other spheres, can work in loftier worlds. For the intelligence is also of the being of the Self, is also part of our essential nature, and in unfolding the Spirit, we develop all that is permanent in us, all that, in its passing reflections, has been to us the source of real joy.

There, then, is the crown of the search for happiness: we find it in the Spirit, we find it in the Self, we find that it is lasting and not transitory, and that neither birth nor death can wrench it out of our hands. If you are sorrowful, it is because the passing has blinded your eyes to the eternal. If you are sorrowful, it is because you are grasping the reflection in the lower worlds instead of the reality in the higher. For know this of a surety, that as there is only One Life in the universe and that Life divine, infinite joy and knowledge and existence rest in that Life, which is ours merely because we live; that Life is Wisdom, that Life is Bliss, that Life is Eternity, and the Spirit in us is of the essence of that Life. All that is joyous has its joy in that Life, and only the blinding veil of ignorance here makes joy turn into pain. It is written in an Indian scripture that wherever you find the Divine Life there is joy; wherever you find joy, there a ray of the Divine Life is beaming; only, in our ignorance, we take the joy in vessels which are brittle, and when the vessels break, we have pain instead of peace.

Realise that all happiness is divine, and then you will know where to hold, and where to let go. Then you will have the test-stone by which is shown the difference between the life which is joy, and the form which is often the source and the cause of pain. Look through the form to the life; look through the outer vehicle to that which is within it; in your friends, in your daily circumstances, in everything around you, look through that which appears to the eye to that which the Spirit knows and feels. Then in the midst of earthly troubles, your joy shall be secure; then in the midst of loss, your wealth shall be safe; then in the midst of trouble, your peace shall be unruffled; in the midst of storm, calm shall remain with you. Build on the permanent, the eternal, the real, and none can touch the joy within you nor change it into sorrow. Have the peace of the heart, and all else may fail you, and you remain content. And remember that this happiness is only yours as you help others to find it; that your life can only know the joy of the Eternal as you feel your life to be one with all lives around you; and that you may never purchase your own happiness by pain to "the meanest thing that breathes".

Printer: G. Subbayya Chetty, Vasanta Press, Adyar.

ADYAR PAMPHLETS

No. 94

Nature's Finer Forces

BY

ANNIE BESANT

October 1918

THEOSOPHICAL PUBLISHING HOUSE

ADYAR, MADRAS, INDIA

Nature's Finer Forces[1]

THOSE of you who have kept at all abreast of the advances of modern Science can hardly have avoided being struck by the very great change that has come over the attitude of Science during the last twenty years. In the days when many of you, and I, were young, Science was dealing with matter, with forms, with all these outer phenomena of nature that can be seen, can be heard, can be touched; and out of the study of these phenomena Science was led to believe in the existence of certain things that could not be seen, nor heard, nor touched. To all these invisible, inaudible, intangible things which caused movements in matter that were not otherwise intelligible, the name of force was given. Matter, it was said, was inert, could not move itself, could not stop itself if set going by something from outside. And it was pointed out in dealing with this inertia of matter that when it was made to move by what was called a force—and force was defined as that which causes movement in matter—it never stopped moving of its own accord, but only by something else that interfered, such as friction. As you know, in ordinary machinery, in the very common instance of the bicycle wheel, you judge the worth of the bearings of that bicycle wheel by the time that it will go on turning after a certain force has set it going. If it stops quickly you say the bearings are not good, too

[1] A Lecture delivered in Australia in 1908.

much friction; so thoroughly is it recognised that matter does not stop moving of itself, but is made to stop by something else, whether it be friction or any other cause. Out of this idea of the inertia of matter necessarily grows the correlative idea of force, as that which causes motion or checks motion, and so Science built up a universe of the two, force and matter. These, of course, were abstractions taken in the singular, and we then have to deal with forces in the plural, the various kinds of things that cause motion in matter. There was, theoretically, one force which might take many shapes, as there was one matter which could assume many forms, and those are two of the fundamental conceptions of modern Science.

In the days of which I speak, twenty, thirty years ago, nothing else was thought by many scientific men to be necessary in order to explain the happenings, the phenomena, of the universe. Matter and force, it was said, were enough for everything. The elder of you will remember the famous book, sometimes called the Bible of Materialism, by the great German Scientist, Büchner. In that book, under the title of *Force and Matter*, the writer dealt with the various phenomena of the world, how the changes took place, and how these, too, were to be considered. I need not remind you, save just in passing, of the definition that was then common for an atom. It was a particle of matter, and according to the author I have just mentioned and his view, which would have been endorsed by other scientists of his own time, the atom was infrangible. When you got down to the atom, you would come to the ultimate, to that which "cannot be cut". That was the notion that Science had at that time, the same idea that had been held for thousands of years, from the times of the great

Greek scientists, and long before that. But in addition to that, it was laid down that this particle of matter which could not be further divided was also unchangeable in its properties. I remember well —for I translated Büchner's book into English—his positive statement that an atom of carbon to all eternity is an atom of carbon, that it has never been anything else, and so on—one phrase after another —showing you how deeply rooted in the minds of the scientists of that time was the conception of an unchangeable atom, which possessed definite attributes, uncreated, indestructible, and that these atoms, with the correlative force which gives motion, were the two things out of which the universe was built up.

Science does not now take that position. One of our leading scientists, Sir Oliver Lodge, wrote a very admirable book, well worthy of study, in which he says there is another factor in the universe—life; that you cannot identify life with force, as many of the older scientists did, regarding life as only the outcome of a particular arrangement of matter, and inseparable from it, disappearing with a change in the arrangement, appearing with an arrangement capable of showing out that force. It would be worth while for the more thoughtful thinkers among you to read his argument, for it is admirably put. He shows in that book that while matter and force make up the universe exterior to consciousness, you cannot regard consciousness as a kind of force, you cannot make life identical with a certain kind of force. Without going into all his arguments, I may put to you the one great fact generally, that force has no direction which is not imposed upon it—bursts out in all directions. It is only when mind comes in and makes a certain apparatus or mechanism that the force is directed in a particular way, as in a pistol or gun your gunpowder explodes, but in order that it may do so effectively, mind has had to contrive the tube of the pistol or the grooving of the gun. In this way force is utilised as well as matter by the over-ruling power of consciousness, of mind, and by very many arguments he buttresses up this statement—a fundamental statement—the one which sees nature not as a duality of force and matter, but as a trinity of matter, force, and mind. It is well to realise that very much of what I have to say to you has a bearing on this view.

But let me remind you, before I take that up, of another change that has come over Science; it used to argue for the existence of force, though invisible, because matter cannot move without it. It is now arguing for the existence of matter as a medium for force. That is, the whole thing is turned upside down. Instead of arguing that there must be an invisible, indestructible force, because matter moves, which otherwise would be moveless, Science now is arguing that we must have matter, for we know of forces and they are moving in something. So that you now deduce matter from force instead of force from matter—a very remarkable change, showing you the line upon which Science is travelling.

How has that change come about? Because Science has been advancing, step by step, from the coarse to the subtle, from the gross to the fine. First, examination was through the avenues of the senses—the eye, the ear, the tactile power. But in their investigations scientists found out that many things were existing which these senses were unable to cognise—things too small for the eye to see, things too far away for the eye to examine—and as they studied more and more closely they found that the human senses are things very limited in range, and that there are a vast number of vibrations that do not affect our senses at all, that to us had not existed because we are unable to answer them. Consequently, to try to improve the eye and make it more effective than otherwise it would be, to make the eye see what by itself it could not see, they invented the microscope, and raised it to power after power, until the very, very minute becomes visible by the process of continually magnifying it, and thus raising it to a size which the human eye is able to perceive. So with regard to the infinitely great, as it is often called, the mighty Universe around us; as the eye could not see far enough, they made the telescope to assist it in plunging into the depths of space. The inventions of the microscope and the telescope are but an illustration of the method of science, climbing up step by step from the coarse to the fine. They made balances so delicate that an infinitesimal fraction of a grain would make a scale depressed, so delicate that they could measure weight to an almost inconceivable minuteness. As Science went on conquering the worlds of nature, the worlds of matter and of force, it was by her apparatus that she made her conquests, and the invention of scientists was taxed to the utmost to make a better apparatus, a more delicate piece of mechanism, some way of putting matter together in order that the mysteries of matter might be further investigated by man.

But now she is coming to a very difficult place. She has gone beyond the region for her finest instruments. Her most exquisite apparatus no longer helps her in the realms into which she is penetrating. She wants to understand ether, and ether is imponderable by the finest of her balances. She has passed into a realm where the intangible, the invisible, the inaudible, are crowding around her on every side, and she dimly senses their presence, but is unable to perceive. What is she to do? Problem after problem remains unanswered because the means of investigation are no longer ready to her hand. She knows that there are things outside her ken. She has found it to be so, even by making improvements in her machinery, and at last, almost in despair, she has had to turn to the one deductive science, mathematics, and she prays the mathematician to discover for her what the senses, however aided, are not able to observe. It is remarkable that mathematics is the one science in the modern world that works from generals to particulars by deduction, and is the only one which is absolutely sure. All others work by what is called induction, from particulars to generals. Induction is very sure if you have got hold of all the particulars, but the weakness of that method is that if you fail to observe any one particular, and leave it out, the whole of your investigation fails. That has been happening over and over again lately with modern Science. She has been discovering that in her inductions she has left things out which she had not observed, and has thus vitiated her conclusions. The conclusions have failed. Arguments which seemed unanswerable, conclusions that seemed irrevocable, have been knocked into pieces by discovering that something was left out, so that the induction failed, and Science is face to face now with all the difficulties she thought she had answered.

You know that there are many people who have a greater extent of sense perception as regards the ear, the eye, the sense of touch, than others. Some people can see more than others with regard to delicate shades of colour. If I took you over to Persia or to Kashmir, I could bring before you carpet makers who would see a dozen shades of colour where you and I see only one. Their eyes have been trained to see delicate shades which the ordinary eye looks at unperceiving, and the extraordinary richness of the Persian carpet, the one in which one shade melts into another, the delicacy of the Kashmir weaving, turn on this extraordinary delicacy of the Persian and Kashmirian eye. They see where we are blind, they see variety of colours where we see uniformity.

It is the same with the ear. Of Oriental music most Europeans say it is flat, but what is called flatness by the Western ear is due to gradations of sounds too fine for the ordinary Western ear to hear, and yields tones which are most exquisite to the trained sense. The Indian can discover delicate gradations of sounds produced by his instruments that are not perceptible to the ordinary European ear, trained to a different scale and to different kinds of sounds. But that is not the only thing that shows us that our powers as regards the senses differ very much one from the other. Any few of you, picked out at random, can hear notes of music, sounded out to you from what is called the siren, an apparatus which yields notes higher and higher, by vibrations of air, shorter and more rapid as it turns. At a certain point most would say that there was silence. You see the instrument whirling round, and say: "It is moving still, but there is no sound." There is really a higher sound, and one man perhaps will say: "I still hear it; it is very shrill." It gives a still higher note, and that man becomes deaf to the sound, and will only see the movement. Another, perhaps, will say: "I can still hear it." There is a very fine sound, until at last the notes grow so fine that no ordinary human ear can hear them at all; yet they are shrilling through the atmosphere; the vibrations are dashing up against your ear. You have reached the limit of your power of hearing.

It is the same with colour. You can see only the seven colours of the spectrum, and all the varieties of colour coming between the violet and the red. But there are vibrations below the red. Science has found them out, and by changing their rate of vibration has brought them within the limit of radiance. There are vibrations beyond the violet. Photographs are chiefly made by what are called the actinic rays, which no human eyes can perceive unaided, but there are certain chemicals which can be put on a sheet so that, beyond the violet or purple, you can see the faint purplish hue which tells you of vibrations too delicate for your eye to catch unaided. All these things go to show that you are in a universe of endless possibilities, and you can only know that to which you are able to answer. You know in the Universe of matter that which you can reproduce, and nothing more. All around you finer and more subtle vibrations are playing upon you. You are absolutely insensitive to them. You have developed no organ which is able to answer them, and hence for you they do not exist. These vibrations have colour beyond the spectrum scale of colour. They are there, but you cannot see them. The vibrations of sound are beyond the octaves of sound. They are there, but you cannot hear them. And so Huxley said truly that if our ears were finer we could hear the sap moving in the trees, and the growing of the grass by the side of the road. There are sounds everywhere, inaudible; sights everywhere, invisible; vibrations everywhere, intangible; and a marvellous universe, which would become more marvellous if only our senses were finer to answer to it, if only we could develop powers that as yet humanity has not normally evolved.

Sir William Crookes has helped us here, and has pointed out, making a table of vibrations, all the vibrations that he regards as present in the Universe of matter; in that table he has marked out what we know of the groups of vibrations: that there are electrical vibrations, sound vibrations, a gap, vibrations of light, another gap, and so on, showing how much we know not, how little comparatively we know. Then he went on to say (and we must remember that Crookes is a Theosophist, who studies from the standpoint of the finer Universe) that possibly these finest vibrations in the ether might be the vibrations by which thought is transferred from brain to brain without the medium of coarser matter, beyond the ordinary methods of communication, and he suggested whether it is not possible that some organ will evolve—rudimentary at present in most, but comparatively active in some—whereby the subtle vibrations of ether-transmitted thought may pass from one to another without the grosser matter. Elsewhere he pictured the universe as it would be if your eyes and mine answered to electrical waves instead of to waves of light. Everything would change. Standing here, if my eyes answered to electricity instead of to light, I could not see you, but when I looked through the wall I should be able to see right into the street; for the electrical currents could pass through the walls, and if my eyes answered to them the wall would be to me transparent as glass, but dry air is a non-conductor of electricity, and if the air between you and me is dry enough, we should be invisible to each other if we saw by electrical waves instead of by light waves. He pointed out that if we looked along a silver wire in dry air, we should see a tunnel through the darkness, the air opaque, the wire transparent. He told us a number of other things of that sort, which would make the world quite different from the present.

It is at the point of the discovery of those finer worlds that Eastern Science, older by thousands of years than her Western sister, can give suggestions which perhaps the Westerner may not be too proud presently to utilise, for the Eastern scientist has gone on quite different lines. What is his view of man? —for it all turns upon that. He regards man as a spiritual intelligence, and he regards matter and force as of one nature, into which that spiritual intelligence comes, in order to study and know it. He does not confuse matter and spirit. Man is the living spirit, and his three great attributes are will, activity, and the power to know. And these three attributes of the spiritual intelligence are used in relation to matter and force, which are essentially one. Then our Eastern scientist says that this spiritual intelligence takes on matter, and makes out of it what we call bodies, in order that he may come into touch with the various worlds of the material Universe. As he puts on a certain kind of matter, he can learn about and investigate all things which are made up out of that kind of matter. It is the same idea, if you notice, that Science has: that you can only know a thing when you can answer it in yourself. But the Eastern thinker says that you have appropriated the matter, and have built it into suitable forms. The ordinary scientist will acknowledge that of the physical body, putting it in a different way. But the Eastern sage goes much further. He says: "You have appropriated every kind of matter in the universe, not only that of the physical universe around you; and as you have a physical body by which you can know a physical universe, so you have bodies of finer matter by which you may know finer worlds; you are normally in touch with three different worlds, the matter of your physical body brings you into touch with the physical world; and the matter of what we call the astral body, or part of the subtler body, brings you into touch with the desire world; and still finer matter, mental matter, brings you into touch with the world of mind.

And then he goes a step further. He says that as you have evolved your physical body, and by that evolved body contact the physical world, so you are evolving further finer bodies, and as you evolve them, you will contact the finer worlds; as you evolve them you will answer to the finer forces, and slowly and gradually you will, in process of evolution, be able to know worlds of finer matter and finer forces, in exactly the same way that you now know the world of gross matter and gross forces, that you call the physical Universe. That is his view of bodies and worlds. With that theory, what would naturally be his practice? Where the Western scientist has made apparatus outside him, the Eastern scientist constructs apparatus inside him. That is the difference. Instead of making microscope and telescope and balances, he works to develop finer bodies, and so obtains a means of contact with the finer worlds. He declares that this is possible, and he tells you how to do it, and he bids you make your own experiments and try it for yourself. He points out to you, as I shall be pointing out to you when I deal with that question, that thought has created the physical organs in which it works, and that similarly it can create finer organs for finer purposes, subtler instruments for the measuring of subtler forces. Now I do not ask you to accept that as true, for the moment, but I do ask you, is it so irrational, or is it not in consonance with what you already know of nature and of evolution?

Your physical eye has grown up to be what it is by a long process of evolution, going on for thousands, millions, of years. Your eye began in a little tiny speck of colour in the body of a jellyfish, which only knew a little change of light and darkness, distinguished dimly between the light and the dark. Imagine the feelings of other jellyfish, if they were able to reason as you can reason, if some adventurous jellyfish had pushed on the development of that little speck, and came back presently to his fellow jellyfish, and said: "It is quite possible to see a great many things that you can't see. I can see all sorts of things running about. I can see all sorts of creatures running around us, and can run away if they want to eat me." They would all say: "What nonsense this audacious jellyfish is talking. How can he see when we can't see? How can he know when we, the wise and orthodox jellyfish, know nothing? What is all this nonsense he is talking about forms and things of this sort? How can we possibly escape when the moment comes for us to die? How can we see when anything is coming, and run away? If he is not a lunatic, he is a fraud, and is trying to get the better of us." and so on. These obstinate jellyfish go on in their own way until nature forces them to evolve.

It is very much the same with all of you with your present powers. You can go on if you like, and slowly, slowly, nature will carry you onwards, until your psychical body has organs as your physical body has organs, and reveals to you a new world of wonderful phenomena that you can study as you study the phenomena of the physical world. But suppose you say: "I will learn by the experience of the past. I see that all these senses have been gradually evolved. I see that the eye has grown through all these stages in an immense evolution. I also notice that as we understand the laws of nature, and begin to work with them, they are our helpers. By them we can evolve very much more quickly. We are not at the head of evolution. Humanity has not yet reached perfection. Why should not I try to evolve a little more quickly by utilising the laws of nature that I know, and thereby increase the speed of evolution for myself and for my fellow men?" That is what is being done all round us with regard to the breeding of animals. How is it that a scientific breeder can, in the course of a few generations, develop in his stock certain characteristics? Because he knows the laws of nature and utilises those that suit him, and neutralises those that don't suit him. In that way he brings about what he desires very much more rapidly. By making intelligence a factor, you can do the same with your mind. The laws of psychology are fairly well known; the way in which the mind develops is fairly well understood. If you deliberately apply psychological laws to your own mind, intelligently, rationally, and persistently, you can evolve it at a pace which leaves behind ordinary evolution. Now mind is the power that shapes matter. You shape your physical body from the subtler world which interpenetrates the physical. You can shape your subtle body and give it the organs whereby it shall contact the subtle worlds.

Meditation is the great way of doing this, and it is by meditation that the Eastern psychologist has developed senses which are able to answer to finer vibrations, which are able to contact things invisible to the physical eye. It is on these invisible things, of course, that all religions are really based, only that they have lost the methods of proving them, of demonstrating them to a sceptical world. The result has been that while those great truths—survival after death, communication with the other worlds, living the heavenly life while still in the physical body—are taught by religions, the method of proving them has been lost. Therefore, when Science challenges them with its experiments, they are obliged to say: "We can't demonstrate our truths to you in a similar way." They feel that they are right; a subtle instinct makes them cling to those ideas, despite all the arguments of Science, but they cannot prove them.

Now, it is just here that Theosophy comes in, bringing some of the old Eastern knowledge within the power of study of the Western peoples, advising them to take up some of its methods if they would know the reality of the things in which they have been instructed, and so be able to face a sceptical world, and prove them by first-hand experiment, and not as simply stated on authority.

Let us see whether we cannot make out a good case for the belief in the finer sight, the finer hearing, the finer forces. Men like Frederick Myers came definitely to the conclusion that we are in touch with more worlds than one. You may remember that in *Human Personality*, a most valuable book to read, he drew a distinction between what he called planetary consciousness, that which we are using every day, and cosmic consciousness, which touches the realities on which religions are based. Western Science is being forced into this position now. It cannot escape it. It has found by its own experiments that there are forces subtler than those it is dealing with in the laboratory, forces that it cannot deal with by its apparatus. Psychologists cannot escape from contacting these things through human brains and human intelligences a little out of the normal. Some abnormal human brains have shown a greater capacity than normal brains to respond to finer vibrations. I will ask you for a moment to attend to that, for it is a point of enormous importance. When you deal with consciousness, you may deal with normal consciousness as you see it all round you, the consciousness of the market place and of the professional man, that by which you and I and all the folk around us communicate with each other. There is no doubt about that primary fact. We all know it. But you have not understood human consciousness, if you deal only with the consciousness that shows through the waking brain of ordinary people. The worlds of sleep and dreams were the next that Science tried to examine. First by trying to work upon the dream state by outside contact. You can read a good deal about that in Du Prel's *Philosophy of Mysticism.* You can experiment, if you like, for yourselves, if you will take the trouble and have the patience. It has been shown that by touching the body in various ways you can produce dreams. One famous experiment which was made in France was touching the back of the neck of the sleeper, and wakening the sleeper by the touch. Between the time of the touch and the wakening—a fraction of a second—the man had dreamt a long story of how he had committed a murder, how he had been tried for the crime, heard the charge of the judge to the jury, been condemned to death for the murder, carried to the condemned cell, kept there till the day of the execution, brought out to the execution, and guillotined. As the knife touched his neck—the touch which started the dream—he woke.

Now that is one of many cases showing that the dream consciousness works much more rapidly than the waking consciousness, and therefore works in finer matter than the waking consciousness. The rate of vibration in nervous matter we know, the nervous vibrations in the brain that correspond with waking thoughts. It has been measured; but if you can crowd the events of a week, of a month, of a year, into one part of a second of mortal time, it means that the vibrations corresponding with them are very much quicker, and would have to be measured by an entirely different law of space and time. That showed the scientific men that there was matter finer than that which they knew, and forces subtler than the forces they had studied. Soon they were not content with working under the old methods; they tried to catch and question the dreamer while he was still dreaming, and threw him into a trance that they might do so. So they used the finer forces of nature without understanding them; for when this eye is so closed in the hypnotic trance that it is incapable of receiving an impression, when, if you throw an electric light into it, there is no movement to close the pupil, then, though the eye is thus absolutely insensitive to light, the man can see much further than he can see through his physical eye. He can see hundreds of miles, can tell you what is happening far away; can see through a closed door, and describe what is taking place on the other side of it. People sometimes say this is mental telepathy. Let me give you an instance and see whether telepathy will explain this far sight, which can be used at a distance of hundreds of miles.

You have all heard of my friend, the late Charles Bradlaugh. He was a materialist, and did not believe in these subtler things at all, but he was a man of extraordinary magnetic power and made a number of experiments in mesmerism. He gave it up because it seemed to have no natural explanation, and he had not the time to make sufficient investigations. One experiment he had made baffled him to the end. He used to experiment by mesmerising his wife. He told me the story himself. One day, in Leeds, I think, he mesmerised her, and said: "Go to the London office of the *National Reformer*, and tell me what article they are setting up." In a moment she said: "I am there. Mrs.——is setting up type." "All right," said he, "look at her, and see and read what she is setting up." His wife began to read the sentence that was being set up by the printer at the moment. She said: "The stupid woman! She has put a letter in upside down." Next morning the proof was delivered to him in Leeds, and he found the sentence his wife had read the day before, with the reversed letter that she had seen put in upside down in the setting of the type. There was certainly no telepathy there; it is not a case you can explain by telepathy, for he did not know it, she did not know it. They were not in touch with the people who were setting up the type.

This case is valuable, inasmuch as it showed the accuracy of that far seeing, and was in itself so trivial. And you can take hundreds of cases of that sort, or experiment yourself if you want to find out about it. Such sight is a simple seeing in finer matter; nothing more, nothing miraculous, nothing superhuman, only a finer organ of vision utilised by the same perceptive power that you use with the coarser organ of vision that you call your physical eye. We call it the astral eye. We call it astral sight. All men will have it after a time. In the long course of evolution, everyone will develop that keener power, and it is very interesting to notice that numbers of people are developing it now, and especially under certain conditions. We find more children born every year with that faculty. In the Western States of America, such as California or Kansas, large numbers of people are somewhat clairvoyant. What is the explanation of people being born with that keener, subtler, vision? One explanation of why so many are being born there with the finer vision is largely climatic. The climate is very different from the climate in Europe, and, I understand, from the climate here. The electric tension is very much higher; the air is filled with electricity to an enormous extent. It is so charged with electricity that if in the winter, when it is cold, you rub your feet on the carpet you can then put out your finger and light the gas. You often see that done as an experiment when, in a lecture on electricity, a person is put on an insulated seat and then is charged with electricity. But in these States no insulation is necessary, and it is a favourite game with little children, rubbing their feet on the carpet as they run, and then making sparks. I have seen it done over there, and have done it myself. You may say: "Why should that make a person clairvoyant?" The electrical condition puts the nerves into a state of higher tension, and they vibrate at a quicker rate. It is quite simple. That is not the only reason. There are other reasons, a number of other things that contribute. But there is one experiment any one of you might make, which will show you how very little is the difference between the ordinary sight and the lower types of the keener sight. I have known people who, when they are ill, become clairvoyant. The answer is that their nerves are out of order, and at a greater tension than it is healthy for the nerves to be. You may say: "Well, then, it is largely the result of disease at present." There comes in the point of the abnormal. As I have said before, that which is abnormal to-day is not necessarily diseased. It may be a case of advancing evolution.

There are two forms of nervous instability. One is the instability of degeneration, on the line of disease; the other is the instability of the growth of a higher sensitiveness, which means advance in evolution. You know how Lombroso and others of his school declared that all cases of genius were cases of degeneration, how they said that genius and lunacy were so closely allied that genius was a disease. Now, if it were true, in a way it would not matter, because everybody would rather have that disease than be without it. One's great longing would be to become diseased, if genius could only be had along that line, for after all one genius is worth a thousand ordinary people to the world. When Lombroso went on to say that all religions, all art, all prophecy, and so on, were all the results of diseased nerves, one felt inclined to go down on one's knees to pray that that disease might spread, for these are the things that make the world worth living in. Now what is the real explanation of this? It is true that these things are abnormal at present. I think we may put it in this way: in both cases the matter of the brain is in a state of what is called unstable equilibrium, and therefore easily thrown off its balance.

As just said, there are two sorts of this instability: one of the instability which goes on into disease and madness, the other of the instability which evolves upwards to a higher stage of human evolution. One goes down into sub-consciousness; the other climbs up into super-consciousness. The man of genius shows you what the human race shall be. He is the prophecy of the future. He is not the product of degeneracy. He shows us what all men shall become at a stage of higher evolution. He is the high-water mark of human progress, and not the sign of a descent. There is, however, much to justify what Lombroso said. It is only fair to admit that at the present time the genius, the artist of the highest kind, the great religious leader, the seer, the prophet, the revealer, has often a brain too delicate to bear the rough vibrations of the outer world as it is constituted to-day. His brain is finer, but is often thrown out of tune, and the result is that side by side with the higher results of consciousness—the answering to the finer forces of the invisible world—you get what is called hysteria, the result of the overstrained condition of the nerves. There is no use in denying the facts. Can they be avoided? Yes. That is the answer of the Eastern scientist. He will say, as Lombroso says, that if you go with an unprepared body to receive these finer forces, they will jangle your nerves out of tune, they will trouble your brain and shatter your nervous system. But there is no reason why you should do it with an unprepared brain or body. Train your brain by strenuous thinking, by devotion to great ideals. Make your brain sensitive to the higher vibrations. But do it gradually. Go step by step. Evolve it slowly and constantly, and then you will be able to receive the finer forces without shattering the instrument whereby they become manifest to your intelligence. Along that line evolution will come. You can train yourself to receive the finer forces, and yet keep the body healthy.

You must refine the body, train it to a finer sensitiveness, at the same time that you preserve perfect health. That is the training by which the finer forces will become your servants, while at the same time they shall not be allowed to disorganise the nervous system, now suited only for the lower forces and coarser types of matter.

Along that line, then, human evolution will go, and you may gradually and slowly build up bodies, developing your astral organs and interlinking them with the physical, so that you may consciously live in more worlds than one, so that you may know that death is nothing except the passing through a doorway from one room to another. For as these senses develop, you will find that the people you call dead are not dead at all. They are more alive than they ever were, living in bodies of finer matter, learning to utilise finer forces. I do not mean that you should reach them by bringing them down here by materialisation, and cross-examining them. I mean that you should reach them by refining yourself, so that you can use the finer body that they wear, and mingle with them in the body that is yours as much as theirs, for you also have astral bodies. You are using them all the time. The only thing you have to do is to assist their evolution, to organise them, to shape the various organs which then will answer to the vibrations outside of finer worlds.

Your friends who have passed through death are only living in the intermediate world first, and then in the heavenly. They are about you, and it is only a question of how much you can communicate with them by means of the finer matter which is part of you now, only you have not learnt to use it. As I said, all men will grow to it in time. It is yours, if you will, to grow to it more quickly. As you evolve by definite gradations, you become more and more sensitive to the finer forces of the subtler world. If this be true—and many of us have proved it to be true by our own experience—Science may begin to utilise these things.

Why do I say "may begin"? Science is beginning already to utilise them, for doctors of the Continent of Europe, especially in Paris, are utilising what we call etheric sight in order to diagnose obscure diseases. They mesmerise the person, and get that person to use the finer sight—for you have all got it—to diagnose the disease, which the physical eye cannot see through the muscle and bones of the physical body; they utilise the X-rays, without the danger of the ordinary use of X-rays. They do not call it clairvoyance. That would not consort with the dignity of the medical profession. They call it internal autoscopy. It does not matter what you call it, only "clairvoyance" is easier to say. They are beginning to use the finer forces. More and more these forces will be utilised. Why should not the chemist use the finer forces to investigate, when his microscope and balance fail? Some of you know that a very large number of important investigations have been made during the last summer. Nearly sixty chemical elements have been examined by clairvoyance, their forms have been pictured, and diagrams have been made, showing the relation of one part to the other. Chemists are interested in what has been done, and at the present time some are studying these things, in order to see how far chemistry can utilise these investigations, carried much further than chemists have been able to carry their researches hitherto. I am not asking that these observations of ours should be taken as facts, only as reasonable hypotheses; that chemists, when they find a mass of information such as

Mr. Leadbeater and myself have been giving them during these late months, entirely made up of clairvoyant observations, should, if they appear to them to be reasonable, use them by experimenting on them. If they can succeed by making discoveries through experiments on these theories, then it will be a fair argument for clairvoyance for us to say: "These things were studied in 1907 by Theosophical clairvoyants, and now Science is proving them." These are possibilities of helpfulness to orthodox scientists.

So with electrical researches. Quite lately I have received—since I have arrived in Australia—a request from one of your own electricians to look clairvoyantly at the X-rays and other rays. Scientific men are beginning to wake up to the possibility of things which a few years ago they denied, and it is the duty of those members of the Society who have developed, to some extent at least, these finer organs, to put them at the service of scientific men, to observe accurately and record exactly what they see. Although I have studied chemistry, I do not pretend to be a great chemist. I realise that what is valuable in these investigations is not the theories which I might make, but the particular facts which I am able to observe. I leave scientists to make the theories, because they know so much more than I know. These are merely actual observations of, to us, visible things. If chemists find they can be utilised to carry chemical science further than it has been carried yet, so much the better. It will introduce them to the higher possibilities of evolution, and make them less sceptical as to the present evolution of man.

You may say to me, and I shall answer straightforwardly: "Is it true that every one has these powers?" Yes. The proof of it is this: There are a few people you find with these powers when wide awake, but you find, if you mesmerise a person, that almost every person can be made clairvoyant. When you stop the coarser vibrations, the finer are able to assert themselves. That is an absolute fact. But just as you would not hear the delicate notes of a violin in the crash of a motor omnibus, so you cannot hear or feel the finer vibrations of matter when the coarser ones are about you, and you are answering to them. The dulling of the coarser parts of the brain enables the finer parts of the brain to be utilised by yourself, the perceiver. If you find that almost everyone mesmerised is able to see, is it not a fair presumption that that is a common power developing in evolution at the present time? Some people have developed it a little bit ahead of others, but all of us will develop it in time. It is only a question of effort applied along a particular line. People, while practically developing it now, require for high success a certain capacity to begin with, just as you cannot make a senior wrangler out of a boy who cannot understand the simple elements of mathematics. And so with any one of you; unless the mental organs are in a state of high development, you must give the senses time to evolve. Though you may not be able to attain it at once, what I want to leave with you is the idea that it is a natural thing. Presently everybody will have it. Whether any one of you can develop it or not depends on your having a little capacity, on having time and patience, by which you will evolve it more rapidly than nature will do it for you. If you will look at things in that way, that you have not reached the highest point of human evolution, that you have to go higher and higher up this mighty ladder, that you have grown out of the mud far below, that you will climb up to the highest point of the Divine Mountain in the days to come, then it will not seem strange that in the past there have been men above their fellows who have spoken of the realities of the other worlds. Then you will realise the possibility of the prophet and the sage. The more highly these powers are developed in you, the more you will grow up to a higher sense of the dignity of human nature; your future destiny will become more real, your inner powers will become to you more possible of realisation; and so the laws of scientific thought, along which I have been trying to lead you, will bring you into regions of beauty, of grandeur, of splendour, that at the present time you can scarcely dream of, and you will know the mighty possibilities which lie in the nature of man, a citizen of heaven, although living for a time on earth.

G. Subbayya Chetty, Vasanta Press, Adyar.

ADYAR PAMPHLETS

No. 95

The Common Foundation of all Religions

BY

H. S. OLCOTT

November 1918

THEOSOPHICAL PUBLISHING HOUSE

ADYAR, MADRAS, INDIA

The Common Foundation of all Religions[1]

BEFORE proceeding with my discourse I must first express the profound thanks of Madame Blavatsky—my learned colleague—and myself for the warm and distinguished welcome we have received, from your Committee on our landing, and this immense assemblage which embraces so large a number of the educated men of this Presidency. We have thus had one more proof of the fact that the progress of our work in India is being watched with affectionate interest by the intelligent classes of the Indian Peninsula. Once more, upon visiting for the first time a Presidency town, we find ourselves among friends the sincerity of whose welcome cannot be misunderstood, and which unmistakably proves that we are not received as strangers but as brethren are who return from a distant land to their own people. Let us hope that the fraternal ties now created between us may never be broken, but grow stronger and stronger as time makes us all to see the necessity for united effort on behalf of the sacred cause of Indian interests. I trust that you will give patient attention to the thoughts that I shall now offer for your consideration.

[1] A lecture delivered at the Pachaiyappa's Hall, Madras, on the 26th April, 1882.

Religion is—according to Mr. Herbert Spencer—"a great (I should say the greatest) reality and a great truth—nothing less than an essential and indestructible element of human nature". He holds that the religious institutions of the world represent a genuine and universal feeling in the race just as really as any other institution. The accessory superstitions which have overgrown and perverted the religious sentiment must not be confounded with the religious sentiment itself. That this is done is a mischievous mistake, alike of religionists and anti-religionists. Science in clearing away these excrescences brings us always nearer the underlying truth, and is therefore the handmaid and friend of true religion. The substratum of truth is the one broad plateau of rock upon which the world's theological superstructures are reared. It is—as the title of our lecture puts it—"the common foundation of all religions".

And now what is it? What is this rock? It is a conglomerate, having more than one element in its composition. In the first place, of necessity, is the idea of a part of man's nature which is non-physical; next, the idea of a *post-mortem* continuation of this non-physical part; third, the existence of an Infinite Principle underlying all phenomena; fourth, a certain relationship between this Infinite Principle and the non-physical part of man.

The evolution of the grander from the lower intellectual conception in this graded sequence is now conceded, alike by the scientist and the theologian. This evolution is accompanied by an elimination, for in religion, as in all other departments of thought, the light cannot be seen until the clouds are cleared away. Primitive truth is the light, theologies the clouds; and they are clouds still, though they glitter with all the hues of the spectrum. Fetish worship, animal worship, hero worship, ancestor worship, nature worship, book worship; polytheism, monotheism, theism, deism, atheism, materialism (which includes positivism), agnosticism; the blind adoration of the idol, the blind adoration of the crucible—these are the Alpha and the Omega of human religious thought, the measure of relative spiritual blindness.

All these concepts pass through a single prism—the human mind. And that is why they are so imperfect, so incongruous, so human. A man can never see the whole light by looking from inside his body outwardly, any more than one can see the clear daylight through a dust-soiled window-glass, or the stars through a smeared reflecting lens. Why? Because the physical senses are adapted only to the things of a physical world, and religion is a transcendentalism. Religious truth is not a thing for physical observation, but one for psychical intuition. One who has not developed this psychical power can never *know* religion as a fact; he can only accept it as a creed, or paint it to himself as an emotional sentimentality. Bigotry is the brand to put upon one; gush that for the other. Back of both, and equally threatening them, is Scepticism.

Like man his religion has its ages; *first*, proclamation, propagandism, martyrdom; *second*, conquest, faith; *third*, neglect, self-criticism; *fourth*, decadence, tenacious formalism; *fifth*, hypocrisy; *sixth*, compromise; *seventh*, decay and extinction. And, like the human race, no religion passes *as a whole* through these stages *seriatim*. At this very day, we see the Australian sunk in the depths of animalism, the American Red Indian just emerging from the Stone Age, the European in the full flush of high material civilisation. And so a glance at religious history shows us the cropping up of highly heretical schools and sects in each great religion, of which each represents some special departure from primitive orthodoxy, some separate advance along the road towards the final goal that we have sketched out. And I also note, as the physician observes the symptoms of his patient, that history constantly shows in the bitter mutual hatreds of these cliques and sects for each other, the clearest proofs that our postulate is correct when we say—as just now—that Religion can never be really known by the physical brain of the physical man. All these hatreds, bitternesses and cruel reprisals of sect for sect, and world's faith for world's faith, show that men mistake the non-essentials for essentials, illusions for realities.

We can test this statement most easily. Look away from this war of theologians to the class of men who have developed their psychical powers and what do you see? In place of strife, peace, agreement, mutual tolerance, a brotherly concord as to the fundamentals of religion. Whatever their exoteric creed they are greater than and far above it, and their innate holiness and gentleness of nature give life and strength to the Church they represent; they are the flowers of the human tree, the brothers of all mankind; for they know what is the light that shines behind the clouds; under the foundations of all the Churches they see the same rock. I ask those of you who wish to be convinced of this fact to read the *Dabistan,* by Mohsan Fani, who records in it his observations of the sāḍhus of twelve different religions two centuries ago. "Granting all the premises"—the modern sceptic will say—"can you prove to me that science has not swept away all your religious hypotheses along with the myths, legends, superstitions and other lumber? Well, I answer, "Yes". It is exactly on that datum line that the Theosophical Society is building itself up. Some people think us opponents of Science, but on the contrary we are its warmest advocates—until it begins to dogmatise from incomplete, known data upon new facts. When it reaches that point we challenge it and fight it with all our strength, such as it may be, just as we fight the dogmatism of theology. For to our mind, it does not matter whether you blindly worship a fetish, a man, a book, or a crucible—it is blind idolatry all the same; and Science can be, and has been, as cruel and remorseless in her way as the Church ever was in hers.

The first step is to have an agreement as to what the word "Science" means. I take it to be the collection and arrangement of observed facts about Nature. If that is correct, then I protest against half measures: I want those observations to be complete, to cover all of Nature, not the half of it. What sort of ontology would it be which, while pretending to investigate the laws of our being, took note only of our anatomy, physiology and whatever relates to the physical frame of man, leaving out all that concerns his mental function? Absurd! you would say; but I ask you whether it is any more absurd to study man in his body without the mind, than to study him in body and mind while ignoring the trans-corporeal manifestations of his middle nature. You want me to define what I mean by this "middle nature" and by its trans-corporeal manifestations: I will do so. I start, then, with the proposition that there is more of a man than can be burnt with fire, eaten by tigers, drowned by water, chopped to pieces with knives, or rotted in the ground. The materialist will deny this, but it does not matter; the proposition can be proved as easily as that he is a man.

They have in Europe a science which they call psychology: it is a misnomer—it is another kind of ology—but we won't quarrel about words. Well, when you come to analyse the Western idea that underlies this term of psychology, you will discover that it relates only to the normal and abnormal intellectual manifestations of the brain. One class of scientists—especially among the alienists, or students of insanity—maintain that mind is a function of the gray vesicles of the lobes of the brain; injure the brain by any one of a dozen accidents, and sensation is cut off, thought ceases, mind is destroyed, the thinking, hence responsible, entity is extinguished. All that is left is carrion, and out of this carrion, before the accident, sprang by magneto-electrical energy all that distinguishes man from the lowest animal, as the lotus springs from slimy mud.

The opposed party affirm that the brain is the organ of the mind, the machine of its manifestation, and that the thinking something in man thinks still and still exists even though the brain be shattered, even though the man die. The one reflects the tone of materialistic science, the other the tone of the Christian Churches and of the two crores of so-called modern Spiritualists. The Materialists regard man as a Unity, a thinking machine, the other regard him as a Duality, a compound of body and soul. There is no ground for a "middle nature" in either of these schools. True, here and there, you will find some casual allusion to a third and higher principle—the "spirit," as, for instance, in the Christian *New Testament* (I *Thessalonians*, v, 23) where Paul says: "I pray God your whole spirit and soul and body be preserved blameless unto the coming of our Lord

Jesus Christ"—an expression which, however sound as theology, is dreadfully loose and heterodox as science. But the whole drift of Christian teaching and of mediumistic teaching favours the duality theory; the body dead, the second principle enters on a new career of its own until it attains to a postulated *summum bonum* or *summum malum* state. Now experienced observers of the mediumistic phenomena have seen many animated figures or more or less substantial apparitions of deceased persons, and these they regard as the returning souls revisiting the land of the living. They have no idea of this middle nature. But the Hindū philosophers make a far deeper analysis of man. Instead of a single part, or a duality, they affirm that there are no fewer than seven distinct groups which go to make up a human being. These are:

(1) The Material body—*Sṭūlasarīra*;
(2) The *Liṅgasarīra*;
(3) The Life Principle—*Jīva*;
(4) The *Kāmarūpa*, resulting as *Māyāvirūpa*;
(5) The Physical Intelligence (or Animal Soul) —*Manas*;
(6) The Spiritual Intelligence—*Buḍḍhi*;
(7) The *Āṭmā*.

And so minute is their analysis, that each of these groups is subdivided into seven sub-groups. Generally speaking, the first, fourth and seventh principles mark the boundaries of the tripartite or trinitarian man. And the fourth, which comes just midway between the gross body (*Sṭūlasarīra*) and the *Āṭmā*, or divine and eternal principle, is this middle nature of which we have been in search. Now the next question to be asked of us is whether this fourth principle, or Māyāvirūpa or human "Double," is intelligent or non-intelligent, matter or spirit; and the next, whether its existence can be scientifically accounted for and proved. We will take them in order.

In itself the Double is but a vapour, a mist, or a solid form according to its relative state of condensation. Given outside the body one set of atmospheric, electric, magnetic, telluric and other conditions, this form may be invisible yet capable of making sounds or giving other tests of its presence; given another set of conditions, it may be visible, but as a misty vapour; given a third set, it may be condensed into perfect visibility and even tangibility. Volumes upon volumes might be filled with bare paragraph abstracts of recorded instances of these apparitional visits. Sometimes the form manifests intelligence, it speaks; sometimes it can only show itself—I am now speaking of the apparitions of dead persons. I have personally seen more than five hundred such apparitions at a place in America where hundreds more saw them, and I put my experiences in the form of a book, which was praised by some of the eminent scientists of Europe as a careful record of scientifically accurate observations. I only mention this to satisfy you that here is no case of hallucination or unsupported statements. Well, then, we have here the middle nature of man acting outside of and after the death of the physical body; though for my part—being a believer in Asiatic Psychology—I do not believe that these post-mortem apparitions are the very man himself—the thinking, responsible Ego. They are, I conceive, but the vapoury image of the deceased—matter energised by a residuum of the vital force which is still entangled in the lingering molecules. But to prove our proposition we must show that this middle principle, this *Māyāvirūpa* or Double, can be separated from the living body at will, projected to a distance, and animated by the full consciousness of the man.

We have two means of proving this—(1) in the concurrent testimony of eye-witnesses as recorded in the literature of different races; and (2) in the evidence of living witnesses. In the Hiṇḍū religious and philosophical works there are many such testimonies. Not to mention others, we may cite the case of Sankarāchārya, who entranced his body, left it in the custody of his disciples, entered the body of a Rājah just deceased, and lived in it for a number of weeks; and that of Agasṭya, who appeared in the heat of the battle between Rāma and Rāvaṇa, while his body was entranced in the Nilghiris. This story is given in the *Rāmāyaṇa*. In Paṭañjali's *Yoga Sūṭras* this phenomenon is affirmed to be within the power of every Siḍḍha who perfects himself in Yoga. As to living witnesses, I am one myself; for I have seen the Doubles of several men acting intelligently at great distances from their bodies, and in this pamphlet that I now show you,[1] will be found the certificates of no less than nine reputable persons—five Hiṇḍūs and four Europeans—that they have seen such appearances on various occasions within the past two years. And then we have the scores of similar attestations from credible persons living in different parts of the world which are to be read in many European books treating upon these subjects. I do not pretend to say that a sceptical public can be expected to take this mass of evidence, conclusive as it may be, without reserve; the alleged phenomenon so surpasses ordinary human experience that, to believe its reality, each one must see for himself. I however do affirm that we have here a case of probable verity made out; for, under the strictest canons of scientific orthodoxy, we cannot suspect a conspiracy to lie among so many individual witnesses, who never saw or heard of each other, who, in fact, did not even live

[1] *Hints on Esoteric Theosophy* (Calcutta, 1882).

in the same generation, but yet whose testimonies corroborate each other.

But if we have a case of probable truth, the man of science will ask us what we next demand of him. Do we allege a natural and scientific, or a supernatural, hence unscientific, explanation for the projection of the Double of the living, and the apparition of that of the deceased man? I answer, most assuredly, the former. I am devoted enough to Science to deny, with all the emphasis I can give to words, the fact that a miraculous phenomenon ever took place, in this agé or any age. Whatever has ever occurred must have done so within the operation of natural law. To suppose anything else would be equivalent to saying that there is no permanency in the laws of the universe, but that they can be set aside and played with at the caprice of an irresponsible and meddlesome Power. We should be in a universe going by jerks, started and stopped like a clock that a child is playing with. This supernaturalism is the curse of all creeds, it hangs like an incubus around the neck of the religions and hatches the satire of the sceptic; it is the dry-rot that eats out the heart of any faith that builds upon it. This it is which, carried in the body of a church, foredooms it to ultimate destruction as surely as the hidden cancer carried in the human system will one day kill it. And of all epochs this nineteenth century is the worst in which to come before the public as the champions of supernatural religions. They are going down in every land, melting before the laboratory fires like waxen images. No, when I stand forth as the defender of Hindūism, Buḍḍhism or Zoroastrianism, I wish it understood that I do not claim any respect or tolerance for them outside the limits of natural law. I believe—nay I *know*—that their foundation is a scientific one, and on those conditions they must stand or fall so far as I am concerned. I do not say they are in equally close reconciliation with science, but I do say that whatever foundation they have, whether broad or narrow, long or short, is and must be a scientific one. And so, too, when I ask you to cease from making yourselves ridiculous by denying the existence of this middle nature in man, it is because I am persuaded, as the result of much reading and a good deal of personal experience, that the Double, or Māyāvirūpa, is a scientific fact.

Well then, to return—is it matter or something else? I say matter *plus* something else. And here stop a moment to think what matter is. Loose thinkers—among whom we must class raw lads fresh from college, though they be ever so much titled—are too apt to associate the idea of matter with the properties of density, visibility, and tangibility. But this is very inexcusable. The air we breathe is invisible, yet matter—its equivalents of oxygen, hydrogen, nitrogen and carbonic acid are each atomic, ponderable, demonstrable by analysis. Electricity cannot, except under prepared conditions, be seen, yet it is matter. The Universal Ether of science no one ever saw, yet it is matter in a state of extreme tenuity. Take the familiar example of forms of water, and see how they rapidly run up the scale of tenuity until they elude the clutch of science: stone-hard ice, melted ice, condensed steam, superheated and invisible steam, electricity, and—it is gone out of the world of effects into the world of causes!

Well then, with this warning before you, my cerebrally superheated young friend of the Madras University, pray do not contradict me when I say that the Hindū philosophy of man fits in with the lines of modern science much more snugly than that of either the supernaturalistic Christian or the materialistic man of science. As we have seen the successive forms of water running up into the invisible world, so here, Esoteric Hinḍū Philosophy gives us a graduated series of molecular arrangements in the human economy, at one end of which is the concrete mass of the *Sṭūlasarīra*, at the other the last sublimation called *Āṭmā*, or spirit. "But how can all these exist together in one combination; is a man like a nest of boxes or baskets fitted into each other, or do you mean to say the scientific absurdity that two things can simultaneously occupy the same space?" This is a side question provoked by the main one, but we must dispose of it first.

I will say, then, that as the thing has been explained to me, each of these several sets of atoms which compose the seven parts of man occupy the interstitial space between the next coarser set of atoms. They are focalised as to their several energies in what the Hinḍūs call the Shadadharams, or centres of vital force, crowned by Sahasrāram, in which Āṭmā is located. This supreme point is in the crown of the head; the others are located at the base of the spine, the abdomen, the umbilicus, the heart, the root of the throat, and the centre of the frontal sinus. The atoms of the *Buḍḍhi* would, then, pervade the interstices of the *Manas*; those of the Manas those of the *Kāmarūpa*; those of the latter those of the *Jīva*; and those of the *Jiva* those of the *Sṭūlasarīra.* And as each coarser contains the particles of all the finer principles, therefore the Sṭūlasarīra is the gross casket within which the several parts of the composite man are contained. Pervading and energising all is the Āṭmā, or that incomprehensible final energy which cannot be comprehended by the physical senses, and which is described to himself by the Brahman in the *Māṇḍūkya-Upaniṣhaṭ* by saying: "Thou art not this, nor that, nor the third, nor anything which the mind can grasp with the help of the physical perceptions." Your popular Telugu poet beautifully and allegorically depicts this idea in his poem *Sīṭārāma Āñjanīyam* (cosmic matter) where Sīṭā—who is herself the personification of Prakṛṭi—is asked by the daughters and wives of the Ṛṣhis to point out her husband, but, through modesty, refrains. The ladies then pointing successively to a number of different men ask each time: "Is this thy husband?" She answers in the negative, but when they point to Rāma she is silent; for she cannot even speak of her heart's lord before strangers. So the poet would have us understand, while we may freely say what Āṭmā is *not*, when we are required to say what *it is* we must be silent, for words are powerless to express the sublime idea.

We have now prepared the ground to answer both of the questions put to us by our imaginary critic. The Kāmarūpa, when intelligently projected beyond the physical body by the developed energy of an Initiate of Occult Science, contains in it all his Manas and Buddhi (including the *Chiṭṭham* and *Ahaṅkāram*—sense of individuality)—his Intelligence and Spiritual Intelligence. The Initiate quits his earthly casket—in which are left the Jīva and Liṅgasarīra—and for the moment lives, thinks and acts in this Double of himself. Its atomic condition being less dense than that of the corporeal body, it has enhanced powers of locomotion and perception. Barriers that would stop the body—for example, the walls of a room—cannot stop it, for its particles may pass through the interstices of the gross matter composing the wall. It is in the subjective world and may traverse its space like thought, which is itself a form of energy. Or, if he likes, the Initiate may simply project a non-intelligent image of himself and make it appear at the spot at which he may have focalised his thought. It depends upon him whether the image shall be but an illusionary form, or his own self; it may be mere matter, or matter *plus* himself. As to our accounting for the middle nature of man scientifically, I have already shown that we may do this by the collection of testimonies, and by personal observation. We may add that further proof is obtainable by the best and surest of all methods—that of going oneself through the necessary course of self-training and projecting one's own Double. For this is no exclusive science reserved for a favoured few; it is a true science based upon natural law, and within the reach of everyone who has the requisite qualifications. The humblest labourer may lift the veil of mystery as well as the proudest sovereign or the haughtiest priest.

But it is constantly asked: why are not these secrets thrown open to the world as freely as the details of chemistry or any other branch of knowledge? It is a natural question—for a superficial reasoner to put; but it is not a sound one. The difference between psychic and physical sciences is that the former can only be learned by the self-evolution of psychical powers. No college professor can evolve them for you, nor any friend, fellow-student or relative; you must evolve them for yourself. Can another man learn music, or Samskṛt, or the art of painting or sculpture for you? Can another eat, sleep, feel warm or cold, digest or breathe for you? Then why should you expect him to learn psychology for you? Anyhow he cannot do it, however much you may expect it, and that is the final answer to all such questioners. Nor is it absolutely *certain* that, even though you should try ever so much, you could evolve these powers in yourself. Has every man the capacity for languages, or music, or poetry, or science, or philosophy? You know that each of these require certain clear aptitudes, and it you have them not you can never become musician, poet, scientist or philosopher. The branches of physical science are difficult to master, even when you have the natural capacity; but psychical science is more difficult than either of them—I might almost say than all combined. That is why the Mahāṭmā has been described as "the rare efflorescence of a generation of enquirers" (Sinnet's *The Occult World*, p. 101), and in all generations the true Sāḍhu has been reverenced as almost a superhuman being. The term applies to him only in the sense of his being above the weaknesses, the prejudice and the ignorance of his fellow men.

With the most absurd blindness to the experience of the race, we Founders of the Theosophical Society are constantly being asked to turn its members into Adepts. We must show the short cut to the Himavaṭ, the private passages to the Asramums in the Nilghiris! They are not willing to work and suffer for the getting of knowledge, as all who have got it heretofore, they must be put into a first-class carriage and taken straight behind the Veil of Isis! They fancy our Society an improved sort of Miracle Club, or School of Magic wherein for ten rupees a man can become a Mahāṭmā between the morning bath and the evening meal! Such people entirely overlook the avowed two chief objects of the Society —the formation of a nucleus of an Universal Brotherhood for the research after truth and the promoṭion of kind feelings between man and man; and the promotion of the study of ancient religions, philosophies and sciences. They do not appreciate this purely unselfish part of the Society's work, nor seem to think it a noble and most meritorious thing to labour for the enlightenment and happiness of mankind. They have an insatiable curiosity to behold wonders, seeing which they would not, in many instances, be stimulated to search after the hidden springs of wisdom, but only sit with open mouth and pendulous tongue, to wonder how the trick was done and what would be the next one?

Such minds can get no profit by joining the Theosophical Society, and I advise them to stay outside. We want no such selfish triflers. Ours is a serious, hard-working, self-denying Society, and we want only men worthy to be called men and worthy of our respect. We want men whose first question will not be "what good can I get by joining?" but "what good can I *do* by joining?" Our work requires the services of men who can be satisfied to labour for the next generation and the succeeding ones; men who, seeing the lamentable religious state of the world—seeing noble faiths debased, temples, churches, and holy shrines thronged by hypocrites and mockers—burn with a desire to rekindle the fires of spirituality and morality upon the polluted altars, and bring the knowledge of the Ṛṣhis within the reach of a sin-burdened world. We want Hinḍūs who can love India with so pure an affection that they will count it a joy and an honour beyond the price to work and to suffer, even, for her sake. Men we want, who will be able to put aside for the moment their puerile hatreds of race, and creed, and caste, as they put away a soiled cloth or a worn-out garment; and with a loving heart and clean conscience be ready to join with every other man—be he black or white, red or yellow, bondsman or freeman—whose heart beats with love for India and her wide-scattered children of many races, throughout the world. We welcome most those who are ready to trample under foot their selfishness when it comes in conflict with the general good. We welcome the intelligent student of science who has such broad conceptions of his subject that he considers it quite as important to solve the mystery of Force as to know the atomic combinations of Matter, and feeling so, is not afraid or ashamed to take for his teacher anyone who is competent, whatever be the colour of his skin.

Now to take our scientific argument one step further. Granted that the existence of the Double has been proven, and also its projectibility, how is it projected? By an expenditure of energy, of course. That energy is the vital force set in motion by the will. The power of concentrating the will for this purpose is one that may be natural or acquired. There are some persons who have it naturally so strong in them that they often send their Doubles to distant places and make them visible, though they may never have given a day's study to the science of psychology; I have known both men and women of this sort. But it is an uncommon power, and can never be exercised at all times except by the true proficient in psychological science. The operations of the brain in mechanically evolving the current of will-force have been more or less carefully expounded by Bain and Maudsley, while Professors Tait and Balfour Stewart have, in their *Unseen Universe*, traced for us the dynamic effect of thought evolution into the Ether, or, as Hindūs have called it these thousands of years, the *Ākāsa*. They go so far as to say that it is not an unthinkable proposition that the evolution of thought in a single human brain may dynamically affect a distant planet. In other words, when a thought is evolved a vibration of etheric particles is set up, and this motion must continue on indefinitely. Now the Yogī evolves such a current and turns it upon himself as a concentrated force; continuing the process until the power is sufficient to force his Double out of its corporeal encasement, and to project it to whatsoever locality he desires. We have thus shown the fact of the Māyāvirūpa, its capability to exist outside the body, and the energy which causes its projection. I cannot go into details to elaborate the argument, for I can only detain you an hour in this tropical heat. But I have at least, I trust, shown you that I rely only upon scientific principles, and claim no indulgence from the advocates of supernaturalism.

And now is this Double—which is none other than what is commonly called the "Soul," immortal? No, it is not. So much of it as is matter in aggregation must ultimately obey the law of dispersion which in time breaks up and forces out of the objective universe whatever is material. It is equally the law of planetary as of lesser forms. As all that is material in a star was primarily condensed from the loose atoms in space, so all that is material in the human body, however coarse or however fine it may be, was primarily condensed from the chaotic atoms in the Ākâsa. And to that dispersed condition they must return whenever the centripetal force that attracted them into the human nucleus ceases to resist the centrifugal force or attractions of the atoms of space. This brings us right upon the problem of a continuity of existence beyond the physical death. Here is the dividing line between the world's religions. The dualists affirm that this soul goes to heavenly or infernal places to be for ever blest or punished according to the deeds done in the body. Though they do not use the very word, yet it is the doctrine of merit they teach. For even those extremely unscientific theologians who affirm that a punishing and rewarding Deity has from all time preordained some to be saved and some to be damned, tell us that the merit of faith in a certain system of morals and discipline and a share in the vicarious merit of another, are prerequisites to future bliss. We may assume, therefore, that merit, or KARMA, is a corner-stone of Religion. This is both a logical and scientific proposition, for the thoughts, words and deeds of a man are so many causes which must work out corresponding effects; the good ones can only produce good effects, the bad ones only bad—unless they are antagonised and neutralised by stronger ones that are good.

I need not go into the metaphysical analysis of what is bad and what good. We may pass it over with the simple postulate that whatever has either a debasing tendency upon the individual or promotes injustice, misery, suffering, ignorance and animalism in society is essentially bad, that what tends to the contrary is good. I should call that a bad religion which taught that it is meritorious to do evil that good may come; for good can never come out of evil, the evil tree produces not good fruit. A religion that can only be propagated at the point of the sword; or upon the martyr's pile; or under instruments of torture; or by devastating countries and enslaving their populations; or by cunning stratagems seducing ignorant children or adults away from their families and castes and ancestral creeds—is a vile and devilish religion, the enemy of truth, the destroyer of social happiness. If a religion is not based upon a lie, the fact can be proved and it can stand unshaken as the rocky mountain against all the assaults of sceptics. A true religion is not one that runs to holes and corners, like a naked leper to hide his sores, when a bold critic casts his searching eye upon it and asks for its credentials. If I stand here to defend what is good in Hindūism, it is because of my full conviction that that good exists, and that however fantastic and even childish some may think its tangled overgrowth of customs, legends and superstitions, there is the rock of truth, of scientific truth, below them all. On that rock it is destined to stand through countless coming generations as it has already stood through the countless generations which have professed that hoary Faith since the Ṛṣhis shot from their Himālayan heights the blazing light of spiritual truth over a dark and ignorant world.

It is most reasonable that you should ask me what those of you are to do who are not gifted with the power to get outside the illusion-breeding screen of the body and acquire an intimate actual perception of "Divine" truth through the developed psychical senses. As we have ourselves shown that all men cannot be Adepts, what comfort do we hold out to the rest? This involves a momentary glance at the theory of rebirths. If this little span of human life we are now enjoying be the entire sum of human existence; if you and I never lived before and will never live again, then there would be no ray of hope to offer to any mind that was not capable of the intellectual suicide of blind faith. The doctrine of a vicarious atonement for sin is not merely unthinkable, it is positively repulsive to one who can take a larger and more scientific view of man's origin and destiny than that of the dualists. One whose religious perceptions rest upon the intuition that cause and effect are equal; that there is a perfect and correspondential reign of Law throughout the universe; that under any reasonable conception of eternity there must always have been at work the same forces as are now active—must scout the assertion that this brief instant of sentient life is our only one.

Science has traced us back through an inconceivably long sequence of existences—in the human, the animal, the vegetable, and the mineral kingdoms—to the cradle of future sentient life, the Ether of space. Would a man of science, then, make bold to affirm that you and I, who represent a relatively high stage of evolution, came to be what we are without previous development in other births, whether on this earth or other planets? And if he would not, he must, in conformity with his own canons of the conservation and correlation of energy, deduce from the whole analogy of nature that there is another life for us beyond this life. The force which evolved us cannot be expended, it must run on in its vibratory line until its limit is reached. And that limit the Hinḍū and the Buḍḍhist, the Jain and the Zoroastrian Adepts, all define as that abstract world which lies beyond the phenomenal one of illusions and pain. Whatever they may call it—whether Mukṭi, or Nirvāṇa, or Light—it is all the same idea; it is the outcome of the eternal Principle of energy after passing around a cycle of correlations with matter. That final limit the Middle Nature as a whole never reaches, for it is material as to its form, size, colour and atomic relations; if we call it the "Soul," therefore, we may say that the "Soul" is not immortal; for that which is material tends always to resume its primitive atomic condition. And the Hinḍū philosopher, arguing from these premises, teaches that what does escape out of the phenomenal world is Āṭmā, the SPIRIT. And thus, while from the Hinḍū standpoint it is correct to say the "Soul" is not immortal, it must also be added that the "Spirit" is ; for, unlike the Soul or Middle Nature, Āṭmā contains no mortal and perishable ingredients, but is of its essence unchangeable and eternal.

The confusion of the words "Soul" and "Spirit," so common now, is perplexing and mischievous to the last degree.

It is no argument to bring against the Asiatic theory of Palingenesis, that we have no remembrance of former existences. We have forgotten nineteen-twentieths of the incidents of our present life. Memory plays us the most prankish tricks. Every one of us can recollect some one trifling incident out of a whole day's, month's, year's, incidents of our earliest years, and one that was in no way important, nor apparently more calculated than the others to impress itself indelibly upon the memory. How is this? And if this utter forgetfulness of the majority of our life-incidents is no proof that we did not exist consciously at those times, then our oblivion of the entire experiences in previous births is no argument against the fact of such previous births. Nor, let me hasten to add, are the alleged remembrances of previous births, affirmed by the modern school of Reincarnationists, valid proofs of such births; they may be—I do not say they *are* mere tricks of the imagination, cerebral pictures suggested by chance external influences. The only question with us is whether in science and logic it is necessary for us to postulate for ourselves a series of births, somewhere, at various times. And this I think must be answered in the affirmative.

So then conceding the plurality of births, and coming back to our argument, we see that even though anyone of us may not have the capacity for acquiring adeptship in this birth, it is still a possibility to acquire it in a succeeding one. If we make the beginning we create a cause which will, in due time and in proportion to its original energy, sooner or later, give us adeptship, and with it the knowledge of the hidden laws of being, and of the way to break the shackles of matter and obtain Mukṭi—Emancipation. And the first step in this beginning is to cleanse ourselves from vicious desires and habits, to do away with unreasoning prejudices, dogmatism and intolerance, to try to discover what is essentially fundamental and what is non-essential in the religion one professes, and to live up to the highest ideal of goodness, intelligence, and spiritual-mindedness that one can extract from that religion and from the intuitions of one's own nature. I regard that man as a mad iconoclast who would strike down any religion—especially one of the world's ancient religions—without examining it and giving it credit for its intrinsic truth. I call him a vain enthusiast who would patch up a new Faith out of the ancient Faiths, merely to have his name in the mouths of men. I call him a foolish zealot who would expect to make all men see truth as he sees it, since no two men can even see alike a simple tree or shrub, let alone grasp metaphysical propositions with the same clearness. As for those who go about the world to propagate their peculiar religious belief, without the ability to show its superiority to other beliefs which they would supplant, or to answer without equivocation the fair questions of critics—they are either well-meaning visionaries or presumptuous fools. But mad, or vain, or stupid, as either of these may be, if they are sincere they are personally entitled to the respect that sincerity always commands. Unless the whole world is ready to accept one infallible chief and blindly adopt one creed, the wisest, the only rule must ever be to tolerate in our fellow man that infirmity of judgment which we are ourselves always liable to, and never wholly free from. And that is the declared policy and platform of the Theosophical Society—as you may see by reading this pamphlet containing its Rules and Bye-Laws. It is the broad platform of mutual tolerance and universal brotherhood.

There must be elementary stages leading up towards adeptship, you will say; there are, and modern science has laid out some of them. I told you that psychology is the most difficult of sciences to get to the bottom of, but still Western research has cleared many obstacles from the path. Mesmerism is by far the most necessary branch of study to take up first. It gives you (1) proof of the separability of mind from conscious physical existence; a mesmerised subject may show an active intellectual consciousness and discrimination while his body is not only asleep but buried in so profound a trance as to more resemble a livid corpse than a living man; (2) it gives you proof of the actual transmissibility of thought from one mind to another; the mesmeric operator can, without uttering a word or giving a perceptible signal, transmit to his subject the thought in his own mind; (3) it easily proves the reality of a power to hear sounds and see things occurring at great distances, to communicate with the thought of distant persons, to look through walls, down into the bowels of the earth, into the depths of the ocean and through all other obstructions to corporeal vision; (4) of a power to look into the human body, detect the seat and causes of disease, and prescribe suitable remedies, as also a power to impart health and restore physical and mental vigour by the laying on of the mesmerist's hands, or by his imparting his robust vital force to a glass of water for the patient to drink, or to a cloth for him to wear; (5) of a power to see the past and even prognosticate the future. These and many more things Mesmeric Science enables a person, not an Adept of the higher Asiatic Psychology, to prove completely to himself and others. I say this on the authority of a Committee of the Academy of France. And then, besides Mesmerism, there are the highly important branches of Psychometry, Odyle, Mediumism, and others that to barely mention would be beyond the scope of my present lecture. Each and all help the inquirer towards the acquisition of "Divine" wisdom, towards an intelligent and scientific conception of the laws of that "Eternal Something," as Herbert Spencer calls it; which you may call God or by any other name you like. Whatever name you may choose for it, the knowledge of it is the highest goal for human thought, and to be in a state of harmony with it the noblest, first and most necessary aspiration of intelligent man. The pursuit of this knowledge is, in one word, THEOSOPHY, and the proper methods of research constitute Theosophical Science.

And thus in a single sentence I have answered a thousand questions as to what Theosophy is, and what the object of Theosophical research. Most of you, like the great mass of Hindūs, have until this moment been imagining to yourselves that we were come to preach some new religion, to propagate some new conceit, to set up some "New Dispensation". You see now how far you have been from the mark, and what popular injustice has been done to us. Instead of preaching a new religion we are preaching the superior claims of the oldest religions in the world to the confidence of the present generation. It is not our poor ignorant selves that we offer to you as guides and gurus, but the venerable Ṛṣhis of the archaic ages. It is not an American or a Russian, but a hoary Hindū Philosophy that we claim your allegiance for. We come not to pull down and destroy, but to rebuild the strong fabric of Asiatic religion. We ask you to help us to set it up again, not on the shifting and treacherous sands of blind faith, but upon the rocky base of truth, and to cement its separate stones together with the strong cement of Modern Science. Hindūism proper *has nothing whatever to fear from the researches of Science.* Whatever of falsehood may have come down to you from previous generations, we may well dispense with, and when the time comes for us to see through our present *māyā* (illusions) we will cheerfully do so. "The world was not made in a day," and we are not such ignorant enthusiasts as to dream that in a day, or a year, or a generation, long-established errors can be detected and done away with. Let us but always desire to know the truth, and hold ourselves ready to speak for it, act for it, die for it, if necessary, when we may discover it.

People ask us what is our religion, and how it is possible for us to be on equal terms of friendliness with people of such antagonistic Faiths. I answer that what may be our personal preferences among the world's religions has nothing to do with the general question of Theosophy. We are advocating Theosophy as the only method by which one may discover that Eternal Something, not asking people of another creed than ours to take our creed and throw aside their own. We two Founders profess a religion of tolerance, charity, kindness, altruism, or love of one's fellows; a religion that does not try to discover all that is bad in our neighbour's creed, but all that is good, and to make him live up to the best code of morals and piety he can find in it. We profess, in a word, the religion that is embodied in the Golden

Rule of Confucius, of Gauṭama, and of the Founders of nearly all the great religions; and that is preserved for the admiration and reverence of posterity in the Edicts of the good king Asoka on the monoliths and rocks of Hindustan. Following this simple creed, we find no difficulty whatever in living upon terms of perfect peace with the adherent of any creed who will meet us in a reciprocal spirit. If we have been at war with the pretended Christians, it is because they have belied the teachings of Him whom they pretend to call Master, and by every vile and unworthy subterfuge have tried to oppose the growth of our influence. It is they who war upon us, for defending Hinḍūism and the other Asiatic religions, not we who war upon them. If they would practise their own precepts we would never use voice or pen against them, for then they would respect the religious feelings of the Hinḍū, the Pārsī, the Jain, the Jew, the Buḍḍhist and the Musalmān, and deserve our respect in return. But they began with calumny instead of argument, and calumny, I fear, will be their favourite weapon to the bitter end. In comparison with the unmanly conduct of my brawling countryman who lectured here the other day, denouncing the Veḍas as filthy abomination and the Theosophists as disreputable adventurers, how sweet and noble was the behaviour of that Muhammadan lawyer who defended Raymond Lully when a Musalmān tribunal was disposed to punish him for trying to propagate his religion in their city. "If you think it a meritorious act, O Muslims, for a Musalmān to try to preach Islām among the heretics, why should we be uncharitable to this Christian whose motive is identical?" I cannot remember the exact words, but that is the sense. The tender voice of Charity spoke by that lawyer's lips, and his words were the echo of the Spirit of truth.

Come then, ye old men and young men of Madras, if ye call yourselves lovers of India, and would make yourselves worthy of the blessings of the Ṛṣhis, join hands and hearts with us to carry on this great work. We ask you for no honours, no worldly benefits or rewards for ourselves. We do not seek you for followers; choose your proper leaders from among your wisest and purest men, and we will follow them. We do not offer ourselves as your teachers, for all we can teach is what we have learnt from this Asia; the Gospel we circulate is derived from the recluses of the Indian mountains, not from the professors of the West. It is for India we plead, for the restoration of her ancient religion, the vindication of her ancient glory, the maintenance of her greatness in science, the arts and philosophy. If any selfish consideration of sect or caste or local prejudice bars the way, put it aside, at least until you have done something for the land of your birth, the renown of your noble race. In this great crowd I see painted upon your foreheads the vertical sect-marks of the Dwaiṭas and the Visishtāḍvaiṭis, and the horizontal stripes of the Sivas. These are the surface indications of religious differences that have often burst out in bitter words and bitter deeds. But with another sense than the eye of the body I see another set of sect-marks indicative of far greater peril to Indian nationality and Indian spirituality than those. These marks are branded deep upon the brains and hearts of some—though, happily, not all—of your most promising young men, the choicest children of the sorrowing Mother India, and they are eating away the sense of pride that they belong to this race and have inherited this noble religion. These are the B.A., B.L., and M.A. brands that the University over yonder has marked you with. After three years of intercourse with the Hinḍū nation and of identification with its thought, I almost feel a shudder when some noble-browed youth is presented to me as a titled graduate. Not that I undervalue the importance of college culture, nor the honourable distinction one earns by acquiring University degrees; but I say that, *if such distinctions can only be had at the cost of one's national honour and one's spiritual intuitions*, they are a curse to the graduate and a calamity to his country. I would rather see a dirty *Bairāgee* who has his ancestors' intuitive belief in man's spiritual capabilities, than the most brilliant graduate ever turned out of the University, who has lost that belief. Let me companion with the naked hermit of the jungle rather than with a graduate who, though loaded with degrees, has by a course of false history and false science, been made to lose all faith in anything greater in the Universe than a Haeckel or a Comte, or in any powers in himself higher than those of procreation, thought or digestion. Call me a Conservative, if you will; I am Conservative to this extent that, until our modern professors can show me a Philosophy that is unassailable; a science that is self-demonstrative, that is, axiomatic; a psychology that takes in all psychic phenomena; a new religion that is all truth and without a flaw—I shall proclaim that which I feel, I know, to be the fact, *viz.*, that the Ṛṣhis knew the secrets of Nature and of Man, that there is but one common platform of all religions, and that upon it ever stood and now stand in fraternal concord and amity the Hierophants and esoteric Initiates of the world's great Faiths. That platform is THEOSOPHY. May the blessing of its ancient Masters be upon our poor stricken India!

J. Subbayya Chetty, Vasanta Press, Adyar.

ADYAR PAMPHLETS

No. 96

Memories of Past Lives

BY

ANNIE BESANT

December 1918

THEOSOPHICAL PUBLISHING HOUSE

ADYAR, MADRAS, INDIA

Memories of Past Lives[1]

THERE is probably no man now living in the scientific world who does not regard the theory of physical evolution as beyond dispute; there may be many varieties of opinion with regard to details and methods of evolution, but on the fundamental fact, that forms have proceeded from the homogeneous to the heterogeneous, there is complete harmony of educated opinion. Moreover, the evolutionary idea dominates all departments of thought, and is applied to society as much as to the individual. In history it is used as the master-key wherewith to unlock the problems of the growth of nations, and, in sociology, of the progress of civilisations. The rise, the decay, the fall of races are illuminated by this all-pervading idea, and it is difficult now for anyone to throw himself in thought back into the time when law gave way to miracle, and order was replaced by fortuitous irregularity.

In working up to the hypothesis of evolution small indications were searched for, as much as long successions were observed. Things apparently trifling were placed on record, and phenomena apparently trivial were noted with meticulous care. Above all, any incident which seemed to conflict with a recognised law of nature was minutely observed and repeatedly scrutinised, since it might be the indication

[1] Reprinted from *The Theosophist*, Vol. XXXV.

of some force as yet undiscovered, of some hidden law working along lines as yet unknown. Every fact was observed and recorded, challenged and discussed, and each contributed something to the great pyramid of reasons which pointed to evolution as the best hypothesis for explanation of the phenomena of nature. Your dog turned round and round on the hearthrug before composing himself to sleep; was he not governed by an unconscious memory from the times when his ancestors thus prepared a comfortable depression in the jungle for their repose? Your cat pressed her fore-paws on the ground, pushing outwards repeatedly; was it not an unconscious memory which dominated her from the need of her larger predecessors encircled by the tall grass of the forest hiding-place, to flatten out a sufficient bed for luxurious rest? Slight, in truth, are such indications, and yet withal they make up, in their accumulation, a massive argument in favour of unconscious memories of past lives being wrought into the very fabric of the animal body.

But there is one line of questions, provocative of thought, that has not yet been pursued with industry equal to that bestowed on the investigation of bodily movements and habits. The questions remain unanswered, either by biologist or psychologist. Evolution has traced for us the gradual building of our now complex and highly organised bodies; it has shown them to us evolving, in the long course of millions of years, from a fragment of protoplasm, from a simple cell, through form after form, until their present condition has been reached, thus demonstrating a continuity of forms, advancing into greater perfection as organisms. But so far science has not traced a correlative continuity of consciousness—a golden thread on which the innumerable separated bodies might be threaded—a consciousness inhabiting and functioning through this succession of forms. It has not been able to prove—nay, it has not even recognised the likelihood of the possibility—that consciousness passes on unbroken from body to body, carrying with it an ever-increasing content, the accumulated harvest of innumerable experiences, transmuted into capacities, into powers.

Scientists have directed our attention to the splendid inheritance that has come down to us from the past. They have shown us how generation after generation has contributed something to the sum of human knowledge, and how cycle after cycle manifests a growth of average humanity in intellectual power, in extent of consciousness, in fineness and beauty of emotion. But if we ask them to explain the conditions of this growth, to describe the passing on of the content of one consciousness to another; if we ask for some method, comparable to the methods observed in the physical world, whereby we may trace this transmission of the treasures of consciousness, may explain how it made its habits and accumulates experiences which it transforms into mental and moral capacities, then science returns us no answers, but fails to show us the means and the methods of the evolution of consciousness in man.

When, in dealing with animals, science points to the so-called inherited instincts, it does not offer any explanation of the means whereby an intangible self-preserving instinct can be transmitted by an animal to its offspring. That there is some purposive and effective action, apart from any possibility of physical experience having been gained as its instigator, performed by the young of an animal, we can observe over and over again. Of the fact there can be no question. The young of animals, immediately after coming into the world, are seen to play some trick whereby they save themselves from some threatening danger. But science does not tell us how this intangible consciousness of danger can be transmitted by the parent, who has not experienced it, to the offspring who has never known it. If the life-preserving instinct is transmissible through the physical body of the parent, how did the parent come to possess it? If the chicken just out of the shell runs for protection to the mother-hen when the shadow of a hawk above it is seen, science tells us that it is prompted by the life-preserving instinct, the result of the experience of the danger of the hovering hawk, so many having thus perished that the seeking of protection from the bird of prey is transmitted as an instinct. But the difficulty of accepting this explanation lies in the fact that the experience necessary to evolve the instinct can only have been gained by the cocks and hens who were killed by birds of prey; these had no chance thereafter of producing eggs, and so could not transmit their valuable experience, while all the chicks come from eggs belonging to parents who had not experienced the danger, and hence could not have developed the instinct. (I am assuming that the result of such experiences is transmissible as an instinct—an assumption which is quite unwarranted.) The only way of making the experiences of slaughtered animals reappear later as a life-preserving instinct is for the record of the experience to be preserved by some means, and transmitted as an instinct to those belonging to the same type. The Theosophist points to the existence of matter finer than the physical, which vibrates in correspondence with any mood of consciousness—in this case the shock of sudden death. That vibration tends to repeat itself, and that tendency remains, and is reinforced by similar experiences of other slaughtered poultry; this, recorded in the "group-soul," passes as a tendency into all the poultry race, and shows itself in the newly hatched chick the moment the danger threatens the new form. Instinct is "unconscious memory," "inherited experience," but, each one who possesses it takes it from a continuing consciousness, from which his separate lower consciousness is derived. How else can it have originated, how else have been transmitted?

Can it be said that animals learn of danger by the observation of others who perish? That would not explain the unconscious memory in our newly-hatched chicken, who can have observed nothing. But apart from this, it is clear that animals are curiously slow either to observe, or to learn the application to themselves of the actions, the perils, of others. How often do we see a motherly hen running along the side of a pond, clucking desperately to her brood of ducklings that have plunged into the water to the manifest discomposure of the non-swimming hen; but she does the same thing brood after brood; she never learns that the ducklings are able to swim and that there is no danger to be apprehended when they plunge into the water. She calls them as vigorously after ten years of experience as she did after the first brood, so that it does not look as if instinct originated in careful observation of petty movements by animals who then transmit the results of their observations to their offspring.

The whole question of the continuity of consciousness—a continuity necessary to explain the evolution of instinct as much as that of intelligence—is insoluble by science, but has been readily solved by religion. All the great religions of the past and present have realised the eternity of the Spirit:

"God," it is written in a Hebrew Scripture, "created man to be the image of His own Eternity," and in that eternal nature of the Spirit lies the explanation alike of instinct and of intelligence. In the intellect-aspect of this Spirit all the harvests of the experiences of successive lives are stored, and from the treasures of the spiritual memory are sent down assimilated experiences, appearing as instincts, as unconscious memories of past lives, in the new-born form. Every improved form receives as instincts and as innate ideas this wealth of reminiscence: every intellectual and moral faculty is a store of reminiscences, and education is but the awakening of memory.

Thus religion illuminates that which science leaves obscure, and gives us a rational, an intelligible theory of the growth of instinct and of intellect; it shows us a continuity of a consciousness ever increasing in content, embodying itself in forms ever increasing in complexity. The view that man consists not only of bodies in which the working of the law of heredity may be traced, but also is a living consciousness, growing, unfolding, evolving, by the assimilation of the food of experience—this theory is an inevitable pendant to the theory of physical evolution, for the latter remains unintelligible without the former. Special creation, rejected from the physical world, cannot much longer be accepted in the psychical, nor be held to explain satisfactorily the differences between the genius and the dolt, between the congenital saint and the congenital criminal. Unvarying law, the knowledge of which is making man the master of the physical world, must be recognised as prevailing equally in the psychical. The improving bodies must be recognised as instruments to be used for the gaining of furthur experiences by the ever-unfolding consciousness.

A definite opinion on this matter can only be gained by personal study, investigation and research. Knowledge of the great truths of nature is not a gift, but a prize to be won by merit. Every human being must form his own opinions by his own strenuous efforts to discover truth, by the exercise of his own reasoning faculties, by the experiences of his own consciousness. Writers who garb their readers in second-hand opinions, as a dealer in second-hand clothes dresses his customers, will never turn out a decently costumed set of thinkers; they will be clad in misfits. But there are lines of research to be followed, experiences to be gone through and analysed, by those who would arrive at truth—research which has led others to knowledge, experiences which have been found fruitful in results. To these a writer may point his readers, and they, if they will, may follow along such lines for themselves.

I think we may find in our consciousness—in our intelligence and our emotional nature—distinct traces from the past which point to the evolution of our consciousness, as the recurrent laryngeal nerve and the embryonic reptilian heart point to the ancestral line of evolution of our body. I think there are memories forming part of our consciousness which justify belief in previous existences, and point the way to a more intelligent understanding of human life. I think that, by careful observation, we may find memories in ourselves, not only of past events, but of the past training and discipline which have made us what we are, memories which are embedded in, which form even the very fabric of our consciousness, which emerge more clearly as we study them, and become more intelligible the more carefully we observe and analyse them.

But for a moment we must pause on the theory of Reincarnation, on the broad principle of consciousness in evolution.

This theory posits a Spirit, a seed or germ of consciousness planted in matter, and ultimately, after long ages of growth, becoming ready to enter an undeveloped human body, connected by its material with three worlds, the worlds of mind, of desire and of action, otherwise called the heavenly, intermediate and physical worlds. In the physical world this growing Spirit gathers experiences of varied kinds, feels pleasures and pains, joys and sorrows, health and illness, successes and disappointments, the many changing conditions which make up our mortal life. He carries these on with him through death, and in the intermediate world experiences the inevitable results of desires which clashed with the laws of nature, reaping in suffering the harvest of his blundering ignorance. Thus he shapes the beginnings of a conscience, the recognition of an external law of conduct. Passing on to the heavenly world, he builds his mental experiences into mental faculties until, all the food of experience being assimilated, he begins again to hunger, and so returns to earth with the elements of a character, still enveloped in many-folded ignorance, but starting with a little more content of consciousness than he had in his previous life. Such is his cycle of growth, the passing through the three worlds over and over again, ever accumulating experience, ever transmuting it into power. That cycle is repeated over and over again, until the savage grows from the average man, to the man of talent, of noble character; then onwards to the genius, to the saint, to the hero; onwards still to the Perfect Man; onwards yet, through ever-increasing, unimaginable splendours, vanishing into blinding radiance which veils his further progress from our dazzled eyes. Thus every man builds himself, shapes his own destiny, is verily self-created; no one of us is what we are save as we have wrought out our own being; our future is not imposed on us by an arbitrary will or a soulless necessity, but is ours to fashion, to create. There is nothing we cannot accomplish if we are given time, and time is endless. We, the living consciousnesses, we pass from body to body, and each new body takes the impress made upon it by its tenant, the ever-young and immortal Spirit.

I have spoken of the three stages of the life-cycle, each belonging to a definite world; it must be noted that in the physical stage of the life-period, we are living in all the three worlds, for we are thinking and desiring as well as acting, and our body, the vehicle of consciousness, is triple. We lose the physical part of the body at death, and the desire-part at a later period, and live in the mental body—in which all good thoughts and pure emotions have their habitat—while in the heavenly world. When the heaven life is over, the mental body also disintegrates, and there remains but the spiritual body whereof S. Paul speaks, "eternal in the heavens". Into that, the lasting clothing of the Spirit, are woven all the pure results of experiences gathered in the lower worlds. In the building of the new triple body for the new life-cycle in the lower worlds, a new apparatus comes into existence for the use of the spiritual consciousness and the spiritual body; and the latter, retaining within itself the conscious memory of past events, imprints on the lower—its instruments for gathering fresh experience—only the results of the past, as faculties, mental and emotional, with many traces of past experiences which have been outgrown and remain normally in the sub-consciousness. The conscious memory of past events being present only in the spiritual body, the consciousness must be functioning in that in order to "remember"; and such functioning is possible through a system of training and discipline—yoga—which may be studied by anyone who has perseverance, and a certain amount of innate ability for this special kind of work.

But in addition to this there are many unconscious memories, manifesting in faculty, in emotion, in power, traces of the past imprinted on the present, and discoverable by observations on ourselves and others. Hence memories of the past may be clear and definite, obtained by the practice of yoga, or unconscious but shown by results, and closely allied in many ways to what are called instincts, by which you do certain things, think along certain lines, exercise certain functions, and possess certain knowledge without having consciously acquired it. Among the Greeks, and the ancients generally, much stress was laid upon this form of memory. Plato's phrase: "All knowledge is reminiscence," will be remembered. In the researches of psychology today, many surges of feeling, driving a man to hasty, unpremeditated action, are ascribed to the subconsciousness, *i.e.*, the consciousness which shows itself in involuntary thoughts, feelings and actions; these come to us out of the far-off past, without our volition or our conscious creation. How do these come, unless there be continuity of consciousness? Any who study modern psychology will see how great a part unconscious memory plays in our lives, how it is said to be stronger than our reason, how it conjures up pathetic scenes uncalled-for, how at night it throws us into causeless panics. These, we are told, are due to memories of dangers surrounding savages, who must ever be on the alert to guard themselves against sudden attacks, whether of man or beast, breaking into the hours of repose, killing the men and women as they slept. Those past experiences are said to have left records in consciousness, records which lie below the threshold of waking consciousness but are ever present within us. And some say that this is the most important part of our consciousness, though out of sight for the ordinary mind.

We cannot deny to these the name of memory, these experiences out of the past that assert themselves in the present. Study these traces, and see whether they are explicable save by the continuity of consciousness, making the Self of the savage the Self which is yourself to-day, seeing the persistence of the Individual throughout human evolution, growing, expanding, developing, but a fragment of the eternal "I am".

May we not regard instincts as memories buried in the sub-conscious, influencing our actions, determining our "choices"? Is not the moral instinct Conscience, a mass of interwoven memories of past experiences, speaking with the authoritative utterance of all instincts, and deciding on "right" and "wrong" without argument, without reasoning? It speaks clearly when we are walking on well-trodden ways, warning us of dangers experienced in the past, and we shun them at sight as the chicken shuns the downrush of the hawk hovering above it. But as that same chicken has no instinct as regards the rush of a motor-car, so have we no "voice of Conscience" to warn us of the pitfalls in ways hitherto unknown.

Again, innate faculty—what is it but an unconscious memory of subjects mastered in the past? A subject, literary, scientific, artistic, what we will, is taken up by one person and mastered with extraordinary ease; he seizes at sight the main points in the study, taking it up as new, apparently, but so rapidly grasping it that it is obviously an old subject remembered, not a new subject mastered. A second person, by no means intellectually inferior, is observed to be quite dense along this particular line of study; reads a book on it, but keeps little trace of it in his mind; addresses himself to its understanding, but it evades his grasp. He stumbles along feebly, where the other ran unshackled and at ease. To what can such difference be due save to the unconscious memory which science is beginning to recognise? One student has known the subject and is merely remembering it; the other takes it up for the first time, and finds it difficult and obscure.

As an example, we may take H. P. Blavatsky's *Secret Doctrine*, a difficult book; it is said to be obscure, diffuse, the style to be often unattractive, the matter very difficult to follow. I have known some of my friends take up these volumes and study them year after year, men and women, intelligent, quite alert in mind; yet after years of study they cannot grasp its main points nor very often follow its obscure arguments. Let me put against that my own experience of that book. I had not read anything of the subject with which it deals from the standpoint of the Theosophist; it was the first Theosophical book I had read—except *The Occult World*—and it came into my hands, apparently by chance, given to me to review by Mr. Stead, then Editor of the *Pall Mall Gazette*. When I began to read that book, I read it right through day after day, and the whole of it was so familiar as I read, that I sat down and wrote a review which any one may read in the *Pall Mall Gazette* of, I think, February or March, 1889; and anyone who reads that review will find that I had taken the heart out of the book and presented it intelligently to the ordinary newspaper reader. That certainly was not from any special genius on my part. If I had been given a book of some other kind, I might have stumbled over it and made nothing of it at all; but as I read I *remembered*, and the whole philosophy fell into order before me, although to this brain and in this body it came before me for the first time. I allege that in cases like that we have a proof of the accuracy of Plato's idea, mentioned already, that all knowledge is reminiscence; where we have known before we do really remember, and so master without any effort that which another, without a similar experience, may find abstruse, difficult and obscure. We may apply this to any new subject that anyone may take up. If he has learned it before, he will remember and master the subject easily; if not, taken as a new thing, he must learn step by step, and gradually understand the relation between the phenomena studied, working it out laboriously because unknown.

Let us now apply that same idea of memory to genius, say to musical genius. How can we explain, except by previous knowledge existing as memory, the mystery of a little child who sits down to a piano and with little teaching, or with none, outstrips many who have given years of labour to the art? It is not only that we marvel over children like the child Mozart in the past, but in our own day we have seen a number of these infant prodigies, the limit of whose power was the smallness of the child hand, and even with that deficient instrument, they showed a mastery of the instrument that left behind those who had studied music for many years. Do we not see in such child genius the mark of past knowledge, of past power of memory, rather than of learning?

Or let us take the Cherniowsky family; three brothers in it have been before the public for eleven years, drawing huge audiences by their wonderful music; the youngest is now only eighteen, the eldest twenty-two; they have not been taught, but have taught themselves—*i.e.*, they have unconsciously remembered. A little sister of theirs, now five years old, already plays the violin, and since she was a baby the violin has been the one instrument she has loved. Why, if she has no memory?

This precocious genius, this faculty which accomplishes with ease that which others perform with toil and difficulty, is found not only in music. We recall the boy Giotto, on the hill-side with his sheep. Nor is it found only in art. Let us take that marvellous genius, Dr. Brown, who as a little child, when he was only five or six years old, had been able to master dead languages; who, as he grew older, picked up science after science, as other children pick up toys with which they are amused; who carried an ever-increasing burden of knowledge "lightly as a flower," and became one of the most splendid of scientific geniuses, dealing with problems that baffled others but that he easily solved, and standing as a monument of vast constructive scientific power. We find him, according to his father's account, learning at the age when others are but babies, and using those extraordinary powers—memories of the past persisting into the present.

But let us take an altogether other class of memory. We meet some one for the first time. We feel strongly attracted. There is no outward reason for the attraction; we know nothing of his character, of his past; nothing of his ability, of his worth; but an overpowering attraction draws us together, and a life-long, intimate friendship dates from the first meeting, an instantaneous attraction, a recognition of one supremely worthy to be a friend. Many of us have had experiences of that kind. Whence come they? We may have had an equally strong repulsion, perhaps quite as much outside reason, quite as much apart from experience. One attracts and we love; the other repels and we shrink away. We have no reason for either love or repulsion. Whence comes it save as a memory from the past?

A moment's thought shows how such cases are explained from the standpoint of reincarnation. We have met before, have known each other before. In the case of a sudden attraction, it is the soul recognising an ancient friend and comrade across the veil of flesh, the veil of the new body. In the case of repulsion it is the same soul recognising an ancient enemy, one who wronged us bitterly, or whom we have wronged; the soul warns us of danger, the soul warns us of peril, in contact with that ancient foe, and tries to drag away the unconscious body that does not recognise its enemy, the one whom the soul knows from past experience to be a peril in the present. "Instinct" we say; yes, for, as we have seen, instinct is unconscious, or sub-conscious, memory. A wise man obeys such attractions and such repulsions; he does not laugh at them as irrational, nor cast them aside as superstition, as folly; he realises that it is far better for him to keep out of the way of the man concerning whom the inner warning has arisen, to obey the repulsion that drives him away from him. For that repulsion indicates the memory of an ancient wrong, and he is safer out of touch of that man against whom he feels the repulsion.

Do we want to eradicate the past wrong, to get rid of the danger? We can do it better apart than together. If to that man against whom we feel repulsion we send day after day thoughts of pardon and of goodwill; if deliberately, consciously, we send messages of love to the ancient enemy, wishing him good, wishing him well, in spite of the repulsion that we feel, slowly and gradually the pardon and love of the present will erase the memory of the ancient wrong, and later we may meet with indifference, or even may become friends, when, by using the power of thought, we have wiped out the ancient injury and have made instead a bond of brotherhood by thoughts and wishes of good. That is one of the ways we may utilise the unconscious memories coming to us out of our past.

Again, sometimes we find in such a first meeting with an ancient friend that we talk more intimately to the stranger of an hour ago than we talk to brothers or sisters with whom we have been brought up during all our life.

There must be some explanation of those strange psychological happenings, traces—I put it no more strongly than that—worthy of our observation, worthy of our study; for it is these small things in psychology that point the way to discoveries of the problems that confront us in that science. Many of us might add to psychological science by carefully observing, carefully recording, carefully working out, all these instinctive impulses, trying to trace out afterwards the results in the present and in the future, and thus gather together a mass of evidence which may help us to a great extent to understand ourselves.

What is the real explanation of the law of memory of events, and this persistence in consciousness of attraction or repulsion? The explanation lies in that fact of our constitution; the bodies are new, and can only act in conformity with past experiences by receiving an impulse from the indwelling soul in which the memory of those experiences resides. Just as our children are born with a certain developed conscience, which is a moral instinct, just as the child of the savage has not the conscience that our children possess previous to experience in this life, previous to moral instruction, so is it with these instincts, or memories, of the intelligence, which, like the innate moral instinct that we call conscience, are based on experience in the past, and hence are different in people at different stages of evolution.

A conscience with a long past behind it is far more evolved, far more ready to understand moral differences, than the conscience of a less well evolved neighbour. Conscience is not a miraculous implanting; it is the slow growth of moral instinct, growing out of experience, builded by experience, and becoming more and more highly evolved as more and more experience lies behind. And on this all true theories of education must be based. We often deal with children as though they came into our hands to be moulded at our will. Our lack of realisation of the fact that the intelligence of the child, the consciousness of the child, is bringing with it the results of past knowledge, both along intellectual and moral lines, is a fatal blunder in the education of to-day. It is not a "drawing-out," as the name implies—for the name was given by the wiser people of the past. Education in these modern days is entirely a pouring in, and therefore it largely fails in its object. When our teachers realise the fact of reincarnation, when they see in a child an entity with memories to be aroused and faculties to be drawn out, then we shall deal with the child as an individual, and not as though children were turned out by the dozen or the score from some mould into which they are supposed to have been poured. Then our education will begin to be individual; we shall study the child before we begin to educate it, instead of educating it without any study of its faculties. It is only by the recognition of its past that we shall realise that we have in the child a soul full of experience, travelling along his own line. Only when we recognise that, and instead of the class of thirty or forty, we have the small class, where each child is treated individually, only then will education become a reality among us, and the men of the future will grow out of the wiser education thus given to the children. For the subject is profoundly practical when you realise the potencies of daily life.

Much light may be thrown on the question of unconscious memories by the study of memory under trance conditions. All people remember something of their childhood, but all do not know that in the mesmeric trance a person remembers much mere than he does in the waking consciousness. Memories of events have sunk below the threshold of the waking consciousness, but they have not been annihilated; when the consciousness of the extesnal world is stilled, that of the internal world can assert itself, as low music, drowned in the rattle of the streets, becomes audible in the stillness of the night. In the depths of our consciousness, the music of the past is ever playing, and when surface agitations are smoothed away, the notes reach our ears. And so in trance we know that which escapes us when awake. But with regard to childhood there is a thread of memory sufficient to enable anyone to feel that he, the mature individual, is identical with the playing and studying child. That thread is lacking where past lives are concerned, and the feeling of identity, which depends on memory, does not arise.

Colonel de Rochas once told me how he had succeeded, with mesmerised patients, in recovering the memory of babyhood, and gave me a number of instances in which he had thus pursued memory back into infantile recesses. Nor is the memory only that of events, for a mesmerised woman, thrown back in memory into childhood and asked to write, wrote her old childish hand. Interested in this investigation, I asked Colonel de Rochas to see if he could pass backward through birth to the previous death, and evoke memory across the gulf which separates life-period from life-period. Some months later he sent me a number of experiments, since published by him, which had convinced him of the fact of reincarnation. It seems possible that, along this line, proofs may be gradually accumulated, but much testing and repetition will be needed, and a careful shutting out of all external influences.

There are also cases in which, without the inducing of trance, memories of the past survive, and these are found in the cases of children more often than among grown-up people. The brain of the child, being more plastic and impressionable, is more easily affected by the soul than when it is mature. Let us take a few cases of such memories. There was a little lad who showed considerable talent in drawing and modelling, though otherwise a somewhat dull child. He was taken one day by his mother to the Crystal Palace, and saw the statues ranged along the central avenue. He looked at them very earnestly for awhile, and then said to his mother: "O mother, those are the things I used to make." She laughed at him, of course, as foolish people laugh at children, not realising that the unusual should be studied and not ridiculed. "I do not mean when you were my mother," he answered. "It was when I had another mother." This was but a sudden flash of memory, awakened by an outside stimulus; but still it has its value.

We may take an instance from India, where memories of the past are more frequently found than in the West, probably because there is not the same predisposition to regard them as ridiculous. This, like the preceding, came to me from the elder person concerned. He had a little nephew, some five or six years of age, and one day, sitting on his uncle's knee, the child began to prattle about his mother in the village, and told of a little stream at the end of his garden, and how, one day when he had been playing and made himself dirty, his mother sent him to wash in the stream; he went in too far and—woke up elsewhere. The uncle's curiosity was aroused, and he coaxed details about the village from the child, and thought he recognised it. One day he drove with the child through this village, not telling the child anything, but the little boy jumped up excitedly and cried out: "Oh! this is my village where I lived, and where I tumbled into the water, and where my mother lived." He told his uncle where to drive to his cottage, and running in, cried to a woman therein as his mother. The woman naturally knew nothing of the child, but asked by the uncle if she had lost a child, she told him that her little son had been drowned in the stream running by the garden. There we have a more definite memory, verified by the elder people concerned.

Not long ago, one of the members of the Theosophical Society, Minister in an Indian State, and a mature man of ability and good judgment, set to work to collect and investigate cases of memory of the past in persons living in his own neighbourhood. He found and recorded several cases, investigating each carefully, and satisfying himself that the memories were real memories which could be tested. One of them I will mention here because it was curious, and came into a court of law. It was a case of a man who had been killed by a neighbour who was still living in the village. The accusation of murder was brought by the murdered man in his new body! It actually went to trial, and so the thing was investigated, and finally the murder was proved to the satisfaction of the judge. But judgment was reserved on the ground that the man could not bring an action for being murdered, as he was still alive, and the case depended upon his testimony alone; so the whole thing fell through.

Memory of the past can be evolved by gradually sinking down into the depths of consciousness by a process deliberately and patiently practised. Our mind working in our physical brain is constantly active, and is engaged in observing the world outside the body. On these observations it reflects and reasons, and the whole of our normal mental processes have to do with these daily activities which fill our lives. It is not in this busy region that the memories of the past can be evoked. Anyone who would unveil these must learn so to control his mind as to be able, at will, to withdraw it from outer objects and from thoughts connected with them, so as to be able to hold the mind still and empty. It must be wide awake, alert, and yet utterly quiet and unoccupied. Then, slowly and gradually, within that mind, emptied of present thought, there arises a fuller, stronger, deeper consciousness, more vivid, more intensely alive, and this is realised as oneself; the mind is seen to be only an instrument of this, a tool to be used at will. When the mind is thus mastered, when it is made subservient to the higher consciousness, then we feel that this new consciousness is the permanent one, in which our past remains as a memory of events and not only as results in faculty. We find that being quiet in the presence of that higher consciousness, asking it of its past, it will gradually unroll before us the panorama through which it has itself passed, life after life, and thus enable us to review that past and to realise it as our own. We find ourselves to be that consciousness; we rise out of the passing into the permanent, and look back upon our own long past, as before upon the memory of our childhood. We do not keep its memories always in mind, but can recover them at will. It is not an ever-present memory, but on turning our attention to it we can always find it, and we find in that past others who are the friends of to-day. If we find, as people invariably do find, that the people most closely knit to us to-day have been most closely knit to us in the far-off past also, then one after another we may gather our memories, we may compare them side by side, we may test them by each other's rememberings, as men of mature age remember their school-fellows and the incidents of their boyhood and compare those memories which are common to them both; in that way we gradually learn how we built up our character, how we have moulded the later lives through which we have passed. That is within the reach of anyone of us who will take the trouble. I grant that it takes years, but it can be done. There is, so far as I know, no other way to the definite recovery of memory. A person may have flashes of memory from time to time, like the boy with the statues; he may get significant dreams occasionally, in which some trace of the past may emerge; but to have it under control, to be able to turn our attention to the past at will and to remember—that needs effort, long, prolonged, patient, persevering; but inasmuch as everyone is a living soul, that memory is within every one, and it is within our power to awaken it.

No one need fear that the above practice will weaken the mind, or cause the student to become dreamy or less useful in the "practical world". On the contrary, such mastery of the mind much strengthens mental grasp and mental power, and makes one more effective in the ordinary life of the world. It is not only that strength is gained, but the waste of strength is prevented. The mind does not "race," as does a machine which continues to go without the resistance of the material on which it should work; for when it has nothing useful to do, it stops its activity. Worry is to the mind what racing is to the machine, and it wears the mind out where work does not. To control the mind is to have a keen instrument in good condition, always ready for work. Note how slow many people are in grasping an idea, how confused, how uncertain. An average man who has trained his mind to obedience is more effective than a comparatively clever one who knows naught of such control.

Further, the conviction, which will gradually arise in the student who studies these memories of the past of the truth of his permanent Self, will revolutionise the whole life, both individual and social. If we know ourselves to be permanent, living beings, we become strong where now we are weak, wise where now we are foolish, patient where now we are discontented. Not only does it make us strong as individuals, but when we come to deal with social problems we find ourselves able to solve them. We know how to deal with our criminals, who are only young souls, and instead of degrading them when they come into the grasp of the law, we treat them as children needing education, needing training—not needing the liberty they do not know how to use, but as children to be patiently educated—helping them to evolve more rapidly because they have come into our hands. We shall treat them with sympathy and not with anger, with gentleness and not with harshness. I do not mean with a foolish sentimentality which would give them a liberty they would only abuse to the harming of society; I mean a steady discipline which will evolve and strengthen, but has in it nothing brutal, nothing needlessly painful, an education for the child souls which will help them to grow. I have said how this knowledge would affect the education of children. It would also change our politics and sociology, by giving us time to build on a foundation so that the building will be secure. There is nothing which so changes our view of life as a knowledge of the past of which the present is the outcome, a knowledge how to build so that the building may endure in the future. Because things are dark around us and the prospects of society are gloomy; because there is war where social prosperity demands peace, and hatred where mutual assistance ought to be found; because society is a chaos and not an organism; I find the necessity for pressing this truth of past lives on the attention of the thoughtful, of those willing to study, willing to investigate. Realising reincarnation as a fact, we can work for brotherhood, work for improvement. We realise that every living human being has a right to an environment where he can develop his abilities and grow to the utmost of the faculties he has brought with him. We understand that Society as a whole should be as a father and a mother to all those whom it embraces as its children; that the most advanced have duties, have responsibilities, which to a great extent they are neglecting to-day; and that only by understanding, by brotherly love, by willing sacrifice, can we emerge from struggle into peace, from poverty into well-being, from misery and hatred into love and prosperity.

G. Subbayya Chetty, Vasanta Press, Adyar.